"I really liked *The Code* and am happy to recommend it. Both humorous and serious, it is well-written in an original voice that offers guys an honorable path to manhood and offers women an essential insight into how their men operate in the world."

W.E.B. GRIFFIN — *The Wall Street Journal* and *New York Times* No. 1 Bestseller W.E.B. Griffin is the author of more than forty epic novels in six series, with over fifty million copies in print in more than ten languages.

* * * * *

"Thought I'd read a bit in Jack Dale's work and wound up finishing about 2 a.m. *The Code* combines two elements — the wit and practical advice you might have gotten from your grandfather — with a large dose of self-help.

"I can see this book being grabbed by middle-aged Dads and Moms, as well as by Geezer-Grandads who would like to say important things to a 14-year old. And, because of swell notes from a well-spoken lady, Carolyn Strauss, the estrogen crowd might well be tacking *The Code* on feminine walls.

"Halfway through ... it struck me that Jack has codified the ancient Texas credo of living the Cowboy Way: "Take care of your hoss before yourself; be kind to women and children; don't never hurt nobody that don't have it comin'."

SAM CALDWELL — Sam's fiction has won awards, including Best Outdoor Story from the Texas Outdoor Writers Association. His book, *Change Of Tides*, a historical narrative of the Gulf Coast, won "Best Outdoor Book of 2001."

* * * * *

"Got a guy? Get this book!"

CHET SISK's books include *Seven Steps To Success I Learned From Homeless People*, *Because You Can* and his upcoming book *Think This / Not That*. Chet's nationally syndicated television program *Welcome To Life Part II* on the Colours Television Network reaches audiences in Malaysia, The Netherlands, Namibia, Hungary, Morocco, Canada, South Africa and throughout the United States.

* * * * *

"The Code — A Man's Rules for Living Life, Having Fun and Getting Dressed, by Jack Dale, is a wonderfully insightful primer for young men, or for old men who just never grew up. The Feminine Perspectives offered Carolyn Strauss at the end of each chapter anchor and validate Jack's simple but important lessons. Any guy who wants to get the girl and keep her has to crack The Code. I'm giving a copy to both of my (grown-up) boys.

ORVEL RAY WILSON is a co-author, with Jay Conrad Levinson, of five books in the legendary *Guerrilla Marketing* series, including *Guerrilla Selling, Guerrilla Trade Show Selling, Guerrilla TeleSelling, Guerrilla Negotiating,* and *Guerrilla Retailing.* The Guerrilla series now includes 47 titles with 21 million books sold worldwide in 61 languages.

* * * * *

"This book is funny, well-written, full of practical advice and very concrete examples. ... in-depth advice — not a bit of it rings shallow. It comes from a life well-lived, with the experience to back up every one of those rules.

"It will put a lot of youngsters out there on the path to becoming a man. I know I will use *The Code* with my own sons.

"As a curious female, I genuinely wanted to know what codes a man lives by, what he thinks is important and why. I wasn't disappointed. You've done all those formative boys out there a great service, especially those who haven't got a Man in their life to help them down the very difficult road of becoming one. You've also let us women in on the rules, so that we know what to look for in a life partner."

SUSAN MONTGOMERY — Writer, mother of two

* * * * *

"Written honestly ... direct and unambiguous ... filled with hard-earned insight and depth. Refreshing in a culture where values and ethical stances are routinely chopped down to five-second sound bites and bumper-sticker slogans. Also helpful to guys in their late 20s-30s. I wish I'd had it when I was a teenager."

JEREMY SIE — Graphic Designer

THE
CODE

REVISED EDITION

THE
CODE

A MAN'S RULES FOR LIVING LIFE, HAVING FUN, AND GETTING DRESSED

JACK DALE

with commentary and feminine perspective by

CAROLYN STRAUSS

carjack PRESS

DENVER

This book is dedicated to the men in Carolyn's life
who make her a better woman,
and to Caelen, Jameson, and seth
who aspire to be such men.

Revised Edition
Copyright ©2011
Jack Dale and Carolyn Strauss
2nd Printing 2018

CarJack Press
Denver, CO

www.thecoderules.com

ISBN-13 — 978-0-983-68381-0

Book design by Scott Johnson

Printed in the United States of America

CONTENTS

Foreword by W.E.B. Griffin ix

Introduction xi

Introduction to the Revised Edition xvii

THE CODE
RULES FOR LIVING LIFE

Rule #1   Think For Yourself. 7

Rule #2   Integrity Is Not Conditional 17

Rule #3   Never Piss Off Anyone In A Position To Spit In
          Your Food 22

Rule #4   If You Don't Know Who The Pigeon Is, It's You 26

Rule #5   Initiate Or Respond Calmly 31

Rule #6   Never Make A Decision Until You Absolutely
          Have To 34

Rule #7   Keep It Simple, Travel Light, But Never Skimp
          On Ammo 37

Rule #8   Question Everything. 41

Rule #9   Always Have A Contingency Plan 46

Rule #10 Always Identify The Cost 48

Rule #11 Feel The Fear But Act With Courage 51

Rule #12 Set High Standards. Marginal Performance Is
          Unacceptable 53

Rule #13 Stop And Correct Screw-Ups Before Continuing 55

Rule #14 If You Have To Throw A Punch, You've Failed. 59

Rule #15 If Something Is Unavoidable, Power Through It
          And Move On. 61

Rule #16 What Cannot Be Changed Must Be Borne 63

RULES FOR HAVING FUN

Rule #1   Always Remain A Gentleman 71

Rule #2   Always Reach Contentment Long Before Capacity. 74

Rule #3   Capacity Is A Moving Target 77

Rule #4   Practice All Things In Moderation, Especially

           Moderation. 79

Rule #5   Cultivate Your Ability To Find Hidden Beauty 81

Rule #6   Close-Ups Cure Infatuations. 85

Rule #7   Smart And Funny With Style Outlasts

           Good-Looking And Cool 88

Rule #8   Fun Ain't Cheap And It Never Goes On Sale. 93

Rule #9   A Gentleman Acts Like He Wants To Be Asked

           To Come Back Again. 96

RULES FOR HAVING SEX

Rule #1   No Means No, So Stop When You Hear It 101

Rule #2   You're Responsible For Your Partner's Pleasure

           And Well-Being 103

Rule #3   What Happens In Bed, Stays In Bed 105

RULES FOR GETTING DRESSED

Rule #1   A Real Man Can Wear Any Damn Thing He Wants 111

Rule #2   Never Wear White Socks With A Suit Or Dark

           Socks With Shorts. 114

FOREWORD

I really liked *The Code* and am happy to recommend it. Both humorous and serious, it is well-written in an original voice that offers boys an honorable path to manhood and offers women an essential insight into how their men operate in the world.

My novels are all based on real people and actual conditions. I served in the military and had the great good fortune to get to know some truly distinguished officers, NCOs, and spooks. It's my pleasure to tell their stories because these are people who served Duty, Honor, Country with courage, integrity, and sacrifice. They lived by an honorable code.

The Code presents just such an honorable code. The ideas it contains are obviously distilled from years of accumulated experience, the examples set by mentors, and personal introspection. Jack Dale speaks directly to the deep part of each individual trying to decide how to navigate an honorable path through life's challenges.

Boys should read and learn from it, "guys" should live by its rules to become men, women should use it to see the world through their men's eyes, and men should give it as gifts to those who could use a little extra help.

W.E.B. Griffin
Buenos Aires, 2010

INTRODUCTION

If you've picked this book up looking for a manual for painting yourself blue and sitting in the woods beating on a drum, hoping to channel the cave man spirit in a misguided search for huevos, close it now, put it back where you found it, and move along without making a fuss. This book is not for you.

If you're looking for a love-song to machismo and a how-to for the adolescent posturing of the movie tough guy with the "bad-to-the-bone" peel-and-stick tattoo, put this book down immediately. It's not for you either, and it will just leave you confused and unhappy.

Each man who is a man has a code he lives by, and it's usually kept informal and unstated. But recently I had a series of conversations about some of the trickier aspects of manhood with three boys. One was a seventeen-year-old named Seth who was rapidly becoming a man and who was planning to venture into the grown-up world of business. I thought he could use a heads-up about a couple of issues he might have to deal with.

The other two were the sons of an old friend. At twelve- and nine-years old, they're both well on their way to growing up to be fine men, just like their father. However, over the decades I've come to believe that girls are women from birth, but boys have to learn to be men. For that reason, I thought a list of some of the rules a man lives by — that is, a beginning definition of a "code" — might save all three of them some brain damage and help them avoid some of the physical and psychic bruises that come from having to figure it all out from scratch. So, I noted down a one-page summary (expanded a bit and included here as The Code), consulted with the younger boys' father, Eric, and passed a copy along to each of the three of them. They all immediately tacked them up on the walls of their rooms.

Other copies were made and began to circulate, and, as they did, those copies ended up tacked up on other walls. Guys of all ages would read intently, laugh occasionally, indulge in some light conversational banter, eventually change the subject, and the talk would move on. Invariably, though, there would soon be the sounds of tack hammers.

Eric's two sons, Caelen and Jameson, seemed happy with the list, but, later, Jameson, the younger of the two, came to me and started asking questions, wanting explanations of some of the more difficult words and arcane rules. The opportunity to discuss these subjects — on the boys' own terms — was valuable and the subsequent conversations with them were the real genesis of this book.

Some of the explanations they were looking for are simple and some are complex. Some even seem, at first reading, to be contradictory. Therefore, I've written brief essays discussing each "rule" and laying some groundwork for why it has been included, where it came from, or how it works with other rules to fit into the code itself. The term, "the code," sounded slightly pretentious and silly to me, though, and I was searching for something else to call it, but Jameson and Caelen quickly set me straight. They got it just right when they agreed with the pirate captain in the movie who said that they're not really rules: the code's more like guidelines. They're smart kids and they liked the term, so, in honor of their contributions to the book, I kept it.

The key concept underlying this discussion is the question of what it really means to be a "man." The answer lies in the vital difference between being an adult and being a grown-up: an adult has matured physically and chronologically, while a grown-up has matured emotionally and intellectually as well. In the terminology I'll use in this book, a guy who has become a grown-up is a man. A guy who has achieved adulthood but has not yet become a grown-up remains just a guy. Some guys become men at thirteen, while others still haven't become men at fifty or sixty. Right now you're probably thinking of walking examples of each.

The code of behavior a man lives by is usually learned from the mentors he accepts, both consciously and unconsciously, as role models. My own role models included a company of strong women: my mother and grandmother and my late wife of 31 years (who had the virtue of being much smarter than I am, but was kind about it) and some of her friends. There was also a company of warriors: my fighter-pilot father and his wingman and their friends, my cavalry-and-infantry-officer grandfather and his friends, as well as other men and women who were poets, statesmen, writers, thinkers, philosophers, artists, scalawags, pirates, adventurers — gentlemen and ladies all — including people I never met or knew but read about in fiction and non-fiction. Not all role models are good ones, however. A boy who accepts Fagin and the Artful Dodger as role models and learns the code of thieves may become a superlative thief, but he is still just a thief. So, there should be a certain amount of winnowing among role models. In fact, one of the rules in the code is that close-ups cure infatuations and that's as true of role models as it is of anything else. It's sometimes surprising to discover that the shoes you're trying so hard to fill once held feet of clay.

The code I offer here is a distillation of the traits I found in the people I admired and decided to emulate as I grew up. These are my rules and my code. You may live by other rules and a different code.

Fair enough.

I offer the following as a starting point for each guy to discard, use, or improve on in his own journey toward manhood, but with a couple of caveats.

One, a woman can be a wonderful role model for a man. A woman can certainly propel a boy well on his way to manhood in many different ways. A woman can recognize a man when she sees one and can almost always distinguish a man from a mere guy after just a few moments of interaction. A woman can adopt and practice the code. But just as a man will never understand at an essential level what it truly means to be a woman, a woman is barred by her genetics from ever understanding what it means at the deepest level to be a man.

Two, no matter what code he lives by or what his sexual orientation is, a true man remains a gentleman, honors his integrity, treats women with respect, protects and aids the weak, and keeps faith with his friends, irrespective of gender. Strength is the hallmark of a man, but it is an inner strength, an inner integrity, an inner reliance on principle, an adherence to an honorable code, a gentleness, and a sense of fairness.

A man is someone to ride the river with; someone you can trust to guard your back; someone you can trust with your money, your wife, or your life. There are far more guys in the world than there are men, and that's a pity.

Since 52 percent of the people on the planet are female, I thought it would be useful to include a feminine perspective on these purely male points of view, so I asked Carolyn Strauss to comment on what a man can expect from women if he lives by a particular rule.

I hope the women who read this book will find it interesting and useful. I hope the guys who read it will find it helpful and instructive, and I hope the men who read it will get a kick out of it and pass it along to someone who needs it.

Jack Dale

Denver, Colorado, 2010

INTRODUCTION
TO THE REVISED EDITION

My great good friend Eric and I have different opinions on what it means to be a good friend. When his special forces/special operations experience is showing and his tongue is firmly planted in his cheek, he claims that a friend is someone who'll help you move, and a good friend is someone who'll help you move a body. I, on the other hand, contend that a friend is someone who'll bail you out of jail, while a good friend is someone who'll be sitting next to you in the cell saying, "Damn, that was fun!"

In the context of a writing a book, however, a friend is someone who'll read it and say nice things. A good friend will read it and give you honest criticism and useful feedback. My friend Miller, who is infamous for thinking for himself, is exactly that kind of friend. When he read Rule #1 for Living Life, Think for Yourself, in the first edition of this book, something subtle about it bothered him. When he finally figured out what it was, he called me on it. He said that thinking for yourself is vital to getting through life without getting saddled with serious emotional damage and an intellectual limp. It's a critical rule, he said, but the example given in the essay lacked gravitas. There are far more important things to think for yourself about than just a little social inconvenience. I agreed and added two examples of just how far wrong things can go if you let others think for you.

While we were at it, Carolyn responded to the new additions in Rule #1, and I made a few other purely editorial changes throughout the rest of the book – missing words and awkward phrases and such – but The Code itself remains unchanged. The explanation of it, however, is better now. A man may or may not need a village to get through life, but being a member of team, no matter how loosely organized it is, can sure help take the sting out of being self-sufficient.

Jack Dale

Monument Gulch, Colorado, 2011

THE CODE

RULES FOR LIVING LIFE

1. Think for yourself. Never trust *anyone* else to do your thinking for you.

2. Integrity is not conditional — you either have it or you don't. Like virginity, once it's gone, it's gone, no matter what you tell yourself afterwards.

3. Never piss off anyone in a position to spit in your food. (Wait-staff, bartenders, traffic cops, judges, bureaucrats, customs agents, border guards, chefs, mates, wives, ex-wives [up to a point], and the like.)

4. If you can look around the table and not know who the pigeon is, it's you.

5. Always initiate or respond calmly so you have room to escalate as needed to accomplish the mission. Temper is a tool, so use it sparingly and effectively.

6. Preserve your options and never make a decision until you absolutely have to — things will probably change.

7. Keep it simple and travel light enough to accomplish the mission, but *never* skimp on ammo.

8. Question *everything.*

9. *Always* have a contingency plan.

10. Nothing in life is free. If you don't understand the cost of something, you're going to pay, or believe you paid, too much.

11. Feel the fear but act boldly and with courage. Mistakes are an unavoidable part of life, so learn from them and move on.

12. Set high standards. Marginal performance is unacceptable.

13. Screwing-up is a rapidly-accelerating iterative process, so stop and correct the problem as soon as possible.

14. In a social situation, if you have to throw a punch, you've failed in so many other ways that you should be deeply ashamed of yourself. To quote the song, "Somebody's going to emergency; somebody's going to jail." Neither is necessary. Both are aggressively stupid.

15. Sometimes a man has to face an unpleasant, dangerous, or repugnant task, but one that has to be done. When faced with the inevitable, don't hesitate, don't complain, don't whine. Just power through whatever it is, get it done to the best of your ability, and if you survive move on.

16. What cannot be changed must be borne.

RULES FOR HAVING FUN

1. A man always remains a gentleman, although the archaic phrase "a killing gentleman" is not an oxymoron.

2. Always reach contentment long before capacity and be the last man standing so you're able to retain enough self-control to help the fallen.

3. Capacity is a moving target. There's no such thing as too much, but there is more than you can handle at any given time, so a man always keeps his antennae up.

4. Practice all things in moderation, especially moderation. Occasionally, you have to cut your wolf loose, howl at the moon, and stomp on the terra. Fine, but pre-minimize the damage by choosing your spots carefully, leaving behind enough cash with a friend to bail you out, and being prepared to accept the full consequences of your actions.

5. Cultivate your ability to find hidden beauty. Ugliness will show itself on its own.

6. Close-ups cure infatuations.

7. Smart and funny with style outlasts good-looking and cool without it.

8. Fun ain't cheap and it never goes on sale. Having fun is important, so figure it into your budget.

9. In all social situations, a gentleman behaves as though he wants to be asked back for a return engagement, whether he does or not. This applies to everything from a fleeting social encounter or a date to a long week-end in bed or a lifetime of commitment.

RULES FOR HAVING SEX

1. No means no, so stop as soon as you hear it. The absence of "No" is not an automatic "Yes."
2. Each participant should focus on the *pleasure* and *well-being* of the other(s).
3. What happens "in bed," stays in bed. A man will never betray a partner's honor.

RULES FOR GETTING DRESSED

1. Ignore the crowd. A real man can wear any damn thing he wants, whether it's "cool" or not.
2. On the other hand, never wear white socks with a dark suit or black socks with shorts.

RULES FOR LIVING LIFE

THINK FOR YOURSELF

❧

"Be a Man and think for yourself," my father told me.

"Right, Dad!" I parroted. *"Be a Man. Think for myself. Right."*

The first part was hard enough. At thirteen, I figured that, if he said it so off-handedly, it must be not only possible, but what a Man did. I was just entering that stage at which everyone apparently expected me to start acting like a Man, but no one would tell me just what that meant and my own ideas were conflicting and vague. As time passed, I started to get desperate for instruction in what was turning out to be a pretty complicated proposition, but there didn't seem to be any common threads I could work from in the opinions I was getting. Everyone I asked to help me clarify my father's meaning, my friends, my teachers, my coaches, my father's friends — everyone — said, *"Be a Man"* as if everyone except me already knew what that meant.

Finally, when I turned fifteen years old and became a sophomore in high school, a schoolmate, a wise and willowy, dark-haired, gray-eyed, fifteen-year-old girl got me off the hook. Amid starshine, moonlight, and the sounds of a midnight river, she whispered, *"Be my man."* I recognized the difference immediately and ran with it. Although this evolved into a philosophical system derived entirely from instincts, nerve-ends, and pheromones, I operated successfully from that admittedly para-mystical model for the next decade or so.

By the time I reached my mid-twenties, however, I had learned that the second part of Dad's instruction was, by far, the more difficult. In the first place, how do you tell the difference between really thinking for yourself and accepting the judgments of others? The older I got, the more people there were who tried to think for me, but sooner or later Dad's words would echo in my head (as if they were a thought of my own, of course) and I would try to think through whatever was currently being handed me.

I say "Try to think through," because at that time critical thinking couldn't proceed until the comforting sense of inclusion that comes from buying into an established dogma had been pushed aside or swept under a pre-frontal — or limbic — rug. Then, finally, I might be able to manage a critical look at the issue at hand, might be able to tell the difference between the snake oil and the wishful thinking of others and the honest insights and wishful thinking of my own. Slowly, I realized the starting place was to ask *"Exactly what is it that makes their thinking any more valid than mine? Do I lack the self-confidence to do my own thinking?"* Well, sure. We all do at first, and that lack is hard to overcome because rising above it feels like hubris or overweening pride.

Another reason this hesitation is so hard to overcome is that our culture has a tendency to present individuals with other peoples' solutions. This tendency is so subversive that there is no part of our mental geography that hasn't been surveyed, cleared, platted, fenced, and paved. We are inundated to the point of drowning by the opinions, rules, guidelines, laws, principles, precepts, prescriptions, morals, canons, and decrees of others. Then there is the broad range of truth, but truth always gets hijacked by established — and establishment — institutions. You can see exactly how and where this happens when you examine the traditional continuum of belief: perception, insight, ideas, understanding, ideology, dogma, and cant.

There will be times when thinking for yourself will make the critical difference between life and death, or between being able to look yourself in the eye in the mirror in the morning and turning away from your own reflection in shame.

In the early 1970s, a researcher in the psychology department at Stanford University set up a now infamous experiment in human behavior known as the Stanford Prisoner Experiment. To study the psychology of prisoners and guards, he asked for student volunteers for a 14-day program. About a third of those volunteers were selected to participate and were randomly assigned roles as either guards or prisoners. They were shown to a mock prison set up in the basement of the psychology building and they all entered their roles. Within six days, however, the experiment had gotten completely out of control. "Guards" were committing abuses that bordered on torture against "prisoners," and the "prisoners" were buying into their harsh treatment, all because someone in a position of authority – the researcher – had given them orders by pre-defining their respective roles. To make it worse, the researcher himself had gotten sucked in to this completely artificial situation to the point that he accepted the unwarranted abuses as "necessary to maintain order." Finally, an outside third party came to observe. She was so shocked at what she saw, she called them all on what was going on, causing the participants to come to their senses. The experiment was subsequently shut down. Other researchers performed similar experiments at other times in other places and found similar results.

The point is that, unless you think for yourself and decide what you will — and will not — do and why, it would be alarmingly easy to find yourself a guard at Auschwitz or Dachau or the Hanoi Hilton or Abu Ghraib doing things you'd never imagined you'd do to other people. A figure of authority giving orders — especially when backed by group dynamics of acceptance of an us/them duality — can be a powerful force, but one you must resist if the orders conflict with your own sense of right and wrong.

Not every important dilemma will have such dire moral and ethical personal consequences, however. Some consequences will be economic or cultural or both, as happened to so many otherwise careful people in the financial and toxic-mortgage crises of the late-2000s.

Millions of people all over the country were convinced to refinance their existing homes, or were convinced to buy more house than they could possibly afford. Some of these people had great credit, good jobs with good incomes, excellent assets, and homes with fixed-rate mortgages at good low rates. Others had no credit at all. Regardless, they were all lured into new mortgages by the promise of easy access to low-cost cash and the thought that it must be okay because everyone else was doing it, too.

In the process, though, they were cheated blind by unscrupulous mortgage brokers and dishonest bankers who lied to them about the terms. No matter what they were told at the closing, approximately 80% were sold adjustable rate mortgages (ARMs). The results were tragic. When U.S. housing sales peaked in mid-2006, prices began a steep decline and the bubble burst, the stock market imploded, home values plummeted, and interest rates rose dramatically (if you could get a loan at all). Had you been one of these people, the interest on your adjustable-rate loan would have adjusted upwards while the value of your home would have decreased significantly. The amount of your monthly mortgage payment would have sky-rocketed and you would have been unable to refinance because of the lowered value of your home. When you could no longer afford to make the payments, you would have lost everything. Many people did.

Sure, they were lied to and conned by smooth-talking profiteers, but how many of them actually read the loan documents? How many of them did enough due diligence to catch the bankers and the mortgage brokers in their lies and discover the real terms, the falsified income levels, the false home valuations, and so forth? Of course, such documents are purposefully designed to be very hard to understand, which is why no one reads them, and they tend to be thrown at you very quickly. But, in a situation like this, two things are true. When they speed up the rate at which the shells are moving, you can be very sure that there's something about the pea they don't want you to notice. Two, because no one reads the loan documents, dishonest mortgage brokers and bankers can get away with telling you one thing and selling you something else entirely.

Your duty to protect yourself and your family from the predators who prowl the economic jungle means that you cannot afford to commit large sums of money without thinking for yourself at least enough to read and understand the contracts and disclosure documents and the deal's long-term effects on your financial well-being.

A figure of authority in a position of trust (if you can't trust your banker, who can you trust?) assuring you *"this is a good deal"* can be a powerful force. But, thinking for yourself requires that you resist those urgings long enough to confirm whether it's a good deal for you or not, especially when the stakes are high. The perceptual problem is that, the higher the stakes, the greater the assurances that *"it's a good deal"* will be, and the more difficult confirming or disproving that fact becomes. The reason they make it so hard to confirm is that most people won't go to the trouble. They'll just throw up their hands and sign what they're told to sign. Then, they live with the consequences.

Most of the time, however, the situations confronting you won't be so extreme. Sometimes, they'll be lightweight social issues like avoiding a little inconvenience or a long wait. In the last century, I spoke at a conference in Corpus Christi, Texas. Another speaker and I were asked to join some others for beer and oysters at a raw bar out on one of the great stone quays (called "T-heads" by the locals) built out into the bay to form the local marina. We sat talking with our hosts, occasionally eating an oyster, quaffing ice-cold pints, and laughing ' til our faces hurt. The other speaker, Tony, is one of the nicest and funniest people I have ever met and he was on his customary roll. Hours passed pleasantly and late afternoon hilarity slowly bumped up against early evening obligation and the party broke up as people drifted off to various dinner engagements. Finally, Tony and I found ourselves alone at the table thinking about dinner ourselves.

We were both new to Corpus Christi and had no real clues to the local restaurant scene. However, just about 40 yards away as the pelican flies (but actually out at the end of the next T-head down the beach) there was a great-looking restaurant. Laughter and music drifted across the water to us, the place teemed with people, and we decided to eat there. Actually getting there was another matter.

After a quarter-mile walk along our quay back to the beach, a half-mile walk down the beach, and a quarter-mile walk along that next quay out to the restaurant, we approached the maitre'd only to hear that the wait for a table was slightly more than two-and-one-half hours. By now we were very hungry and faced with another quarter-mile walk back down the quay before we could even think about finding another restaurant. The crowd was stacked three deep at the bar as we pondered our predicament. In a sudden moment of criminal clarity, I realized it was just another box to think outside of and asked Tony to come find me if I wasn't back within five or six minutes.

I began to wander through the dining rooms, not completely sure of what I was looking for. However, very quickly I made eye contact with a young couple just finishing dinner, enjoying each other, and so in no hurry to leave. They smiled back and I walked over, introduced myself, and asked if I could talk with them for a moment. They assented and I sat down in one of the extra chairs. When I was seated, we exchanged pleasantries for a minute or two before I asked if they would allow me to buy them dessert and a glass of port in return for their company and conversation. They were a little unsure about what I was up to, but couldn't see any immediate harm from the smiling stranger and so they accepted. Just about that time, Tony spotted me and came over to see what was going on. I introduced him to our new friends and invited him to sit.

When the waitress came over, I asked her to put dessert on my check, the couple ordered, and Tony and I ordered wine and hors d'oeuvres. When the young couple had finished, we exchanged goodbyes and they left. The waitress came to clear their dishes. I thanked her, saying that Tony and I were now ready to order dinner. She gave me a long look. I smiled back. She shrugged and took our orders.

There are always far more solutions to a problem than the ones other people will offer you if you just think for yourself, although I will admit that at some socio-egalitarian level waiting the two-and-a-half hours might have been the *proper* thing to do. But, as Katherine Hepburn is said to have said, *"If you obey all the rules, you miss all the fun."*

Consider that in the 10th Century, almost everything the scientific and other experts thought about how the world works was wrong. Dead wrong! Think about that for a minute and ponder how much of current conventional wisdom will be thought quaint, if not actually wrong, by people a thousand years from today.

As a man, you will find that there are times when you can't afford to — or don't wish to — do the proper thing and meekly sit still for the two-and-a-half hour wait for a table. It is crucial that you weigh the social implications of your options, but then you have to trust your own intellect, make your own decisions, and live with the consequences.

Fortunately, we each have the power to think for ourselves and to see through artifice and surface trappings to understand people, situations, and things as they really are. To be a man — especially your own man — you have to be able to think originally and critically, if possible, but certainly for yourself. If you can't or won't, you'll have to learn to live with being just a guy, and, quite possibly, being everybody else's pigeon.

CAROLYN'S COMMENTARY
ATTRACTION ALERT!

❦

Think for yourself is not just a rule for men, but for anyone who's gotten past playground age. The challenge with following this rule is that it takes time, energy, and a willingness to do some work whenever evaluating roles that have been defined for you by others, documents intended by others to overwhelm you, and anything else presented to you that you haven't designed yourself.

That said, the kind of social boldness it took to approach the couple in the restaurant is very appealing to women, because women are charmed by a confident, humorous, respectful approach and they appreciate the willingness of a man to take a risk and accept possible failure and embarrassment. But more than that, a man who thinks for himself is <u>inherently</u> interesting and, therefore, <u>very</u> attractive to women.

INTEGRITY IS NOT CONDITIONAL

Integrity is not conditional. You either have it or you don't. Like virginity, once it's gone, it's gone, no matter what you tell yourself afterwards. Integrity is the foundation upon which you build ethics, morality, character, and your reputation. Integrity is what allows you to do the right thing, even when it's not in your own best interests. Integrity is what makes you give back the wallet you found on the sidewalk with all the cash still in it. Integrity is what makes your word something others can trust and depend on — not just sometimes, but always. Integrity is not conditional.

Your integrity keeps you ethical and probably moral as well, although I make a firm distinction between ethics and morals. Ethics are a set of secular rules for equitable behavior as distinguished from morals, which are a set of religious rules for virtuous behavior.

I am unwilling to say that religion bestows ethics, because a religion is a fully-formed set of beliefs specifically designed to be taken whole and on faith. Most religions posit some sort of punishment for immoral behavior, whether it's bad karma (the universe is going to do to you as you do to others) or hellfire and damnation (God's going to roast you in hell for eternity).

Ethics, as I'm defining them here, don't spring from fear of punishment, but from a conscious decision to be fair and just and from a good character and personal integrity. But no matter where ethics come from, there are no exceptions to the requirement that you guard your integrity by keeping your word and behaving ethically.

It means things like keeping your hands to yourself and respecting a lady's right to choose, even when the wine hits her wrong and you drive her home because she's completely incapacitated. It means showing up on time when you make an appointment or a date and calling if you are unavoidably delayed. It means not becoming involved with a friend's girlfriend behind his back, even though she lifts both her eyebrows and her skirt for you. It means recording every stroke when you're playing golf and never, ever kicking your ball to a better lie.

Integrity means that your word is trustworthy and that you are, too. Integrity is the yardstick people will use to decide whether or not to associate with you or to work with you. I once asked an executive about the wisdom of doing business with a mutual acquaintance but was warned off when the guy was described as having *"integrity to the extent of his options."*

But having integrity does not mean that you have to tell everything you know. In fact, under the right circumstances, your integrity will prevent you from telling what you know. At other times, having integrity is perfectly compatible with telling complete and outrageous lies, as long as everyone knows at some level that's what they are.

For instance, fly fishing is based on deception, since the basis of the sport is presenting a bit of string, fur, and feathers wrapped cunningly on a steel hook and swearing to the trout by everything you do that it's a real insect and good to eat. That's not only a lie, it's a damned lie by any definition. Worse, when other anglers ask you how you did, you find yourself saying things like, *"Oh, I got my share,"* whether you caught 60 fish or got completely skunked. When they ask you where you caught them, you'll hear yourself say something like, *"Up on Cigar Creek,"* or *"The north fork of the Habañero River"* when you know there are no such places on any map. You are setting out to deceive, mislead, and misdirect the other anglers. Deception is such a way of life for a fly fisher that you just can't stop! Fortunately, every-body knows that anglers are congenitally unable to tell the truth. Part of the fun is in the inventiveness of the lies.

The difference is that this sort of lying is in fun and it's meant to deflect rather than deceive outright because everybody's more or less in on the joke. It's just like a group of people sitting around telling tall tales. If they told the absolute truth of what actually hap-pened, they'd all be bored to tears in about 10 minutes.

What it comes down to is this: if people are depending on your word, it's okay to be wrong, but it's not okay to lie. But just because they are depending on your word doesn't mean you have to give them the information they're seeking. If it's a woman depending on your word, you have to be particularly attentive to the key differences among telling the truth, lying, and deflecting because women don't interact with other women the way men interact with other men. They don't think like we do, and they don't understand how we think. If you tell them anything other than the unvarnished truth, they're going to think (on their terms) that you lied to them, so any information you give them must be true, unless it's one of those situations in which everybody is in on the joke and you're dead certain they are too. But more than that, you can't tell them the truth with the foreknowledge and intention of deceiving them. It's too easy, it's not right, and they don't get the joke the way a man would.

Integrity is not conditional. You either have it or you don't, and that applies to other people you'll meet as well. They either have it or they don't. The downside is that true integrity is a rare commodity, so you'll get lied to and misled a lot. The upside is that all these truths make integrity a handy yardstick for measuring both the people you want to have as your friends, and the people you're glad to accept as your enemies.

CAROLYN'S COMMENTARY
ATTRACTION ALERT!

❧

Trust is crucial to the success of any long-term relationship. A male whose integrity can be trusted is inherently attractive to women, partly because single women seem to see so few of them. If you ask single women about men, many will say that men lie. They're wrong, of course, because men don't lie. Guys, however, do, and they see far more guys than men and that's who they're referring to. Sometimes, of course, it's in a context in which everyone is "in on the joke," which is fine, as long as "everyone" includes the woman the guy is talking to. Men who have integrity, do what they believe is right, are true to their word, and show up trustworthy are very attractive to women, and grown women will choose such men over mere guys every time they can be found.

RULE FOR LIFE #3

NEVER PISS OFF ANYONE
IN A POSITION TO SPIT IN YOUR FOOD

⁓

If any rule should be self-explanatory, it's this one, for two reasons. The first is the practical one.

The most difficult jobs to do day after day are the ones that require you to serve the great American public because, although most people are easy to deal with, some aren't. Some people apparently think it's okay to be demanding, arrogant, cranky, supercilious, rude, inappropriate, downright foul, and so on. Serving them in the name of an employer while maintaining a professional attitude requires great patience, tact, self-control, and a very thick skin. People who can pull that off regularly without slitting throats deserve respect. The final words on good wait-staff and bartenders were spoken by the comic actor, Dudley Moore, in the movie "Arthur," when he said, *"Waiters are just like Santa Claus. You ask them for things and they bring them to you. Aren't they wonderful?"* Yes, Arthur, they are, and the better you treat them, the better the service they provide.

The real question, however, is why in the world would anyone think it was smart, or even okay, to make life worse for anyone, much less the people who are serving them food? Do they think phlegm adds spice to the soup or a piquant charm to the salad?

Nevertheless, people can be outrageous. Here's a classic story from a lady who trains flight attendants for a major airline. One day while she was still flying, she was working the first class cabin on a transatlantic flight. One couple, obviously man and wife, kept up a steady stream of requests, but every time she addressed a question or remark to the wife, the husband answered. When he finally got up to go to the head, she stopped him and said, *"I'm not only here to serve you. I'm also responsible for your safety in case something happens. Is there something about your wife I should know?"*

"What do you mean?" he said.

"Well, every time I ask her a question, you answer. Does she have a condition I should know about?"

"Oh, that," he said. *"No, she just doesn't speak to domestics."*

That was an outrageous thing to say and it makes me wonder what kind of awful things they've consumed with their food.

In America, we live in an outwardly egalitarian society and it doesn't cost a thing to be polite and a bit grateful to people who are earning their livings by serving you.

The second reason to follow this rule is the philosophical one.

Everyone deserves respect until they don't. But, you're never the one who gets to decide. That decision always rests with the other people you're dealing with. People will show you very clearly whether or not they deserve respect by how they deal with you. If other people show you re-spect, you owe it to yourself to return that respect and treat them with courtesy. Otherwise, feel free to be every bit as offensive and rude as they are, or, better yet, to let your wolf off the leash and really show 'em how it's done in the major leagues.

Unless!

Unless the other person is a petty bureaucrat with the power to make your life miserable. Then, you can use this rule to keep your food phlegm-free, retain your freedom, and keep your average bureaucratic wait-time to under three hours. You can also use it to stay on good work-ing terms with assistants, partners, flight attendants, traffic cops, lawyers, auditors, judges, magistrates, IRS agents, boards of directors, customs and other officials of many nations, and your intimate other.

If you really need to see whether or not this rule is necessary, just wait until the next time you get stopped for a traffic violation. Jump out of the car, wave your arms wildly, and scream at the cop, *"I'll have your badge for this, you scum-sucking moron. I'm a taxpayer and you work for me!"* If you're dumb enough to try it, you'll be a lot smarter when you finally get out of jail, and you'll have a very clear idea of exactly why you should never piss off anyone in a position to spit in your food.

CAROLYN'S COMMENTARY

This rule is a man's rule because women don't think this way. On an innate level, most women need to be liked and this rule is a lovely reminder of the need for mutual respect and respect for all. To take this rule one step further, when a minor bureaucrat is in charge of a small portion of your life or when a wife, girlfriend, or any woman is serving you food, drinks, or anything else — anything — remember, spit is mild. Be nice.

IF YOU DON'T KNOW
WHO THE PIGEON IS, IT'S YOU

Life is like one long poker game played with total strangers who come and go from a table with an infinite number of chairs. It's just another little bit of cosmic truth that, where there's a poker table, you can be sure there's at least one pigeon, that is, a person who is easily fooled, easily cheated, or easily controlled. If you look around the table and cannot identify the pigeon, you're it.

The only way you can keep from being everybody/anybody else's pigeon is to know the rules of the game. The only way to know the rules of the game is to seek them out, because nobody will tell you straight up what they are. Either they don't know or everybody needs a pigeon and wising up a pigeon is a losing proposition. After all, as I said earlier, a fool and his money are some party, and people do like parties.

Seeking out the rules of the game means having the curiosity to work at understanding enough of the small pieces of the puzzles of life to find the overview that tells you how they all fit together. The search for the overview is a lifelong process, and the only way to get it is to become a perpetual student.

The perpetual student has the grinding, itching, tormenting compulsion to understand it all, or, at least as much of it as possible. As a result, the perpetual student has to get good at direct research: finding and evaluating information to answer specific questions. The perpetual student has to get good at figuring out if information is trustworthy intel or just someone blowing sunshine up your kilt ... and why they might be going to all the trouble.

The perpetual student has to get very good at indirect or general research: reading, thinking, conversing or writing to understand those thoughts, and just generally paying attention with all antennae up and a finger on the pulse of the world. As the small pieces and solutions to the small puzzles begin to build much as a coral reef does, the perpetual student begins to build an overview.

The overview is the most vital and useful view of the world a person can get. The term is shorthand for a broad, comprehensive perception and understanding of the way the world actually works, the way in which everything in the world is connected to everything else, and the ability to perceive enough of those connections to anticipate and prevent problems before they appear, or to solve them when they show up. The overview is the strategic view that gives a man a fighting chance.

The overview has a Zen quality to it. Getting "it" sounds like *"AHA! So that's how it all fits together,"* and feels like *"So THAT's what that meant."* The person with an overview knows that there's no such thing as thinking outside the box, because there is no box unless you've built it yourself. A person with the overview listens with more understanding than others do, identifies opportunities others miss, recognizes others' motivations and threats more readily, identifies and asks the right questions, and finds more — and more interesting — openings.

The person with an overview knows not to confuse an explanation of causes with a justification of results. The person with an overview knows not to mistake mere correlations for causes, or confuse proximate causes with primary causes.

At its upper limits, the overview is also known as Enlightenment, but unless you were born with the perceptive wisdom of the Buddha, you're going to have to work for it and that means becoming the perpetual student. Fortunately, How The World Really Works is a fascinating subject with practical returns. The choice a man has to make is whether he wants to work hard enough at it that he can sit at the poker table and be pretty sure what's in everyone else's hand, or wants to just sit there as everyone else's pigeon because it's easier than thinking.

CAROLYN'S COMMENTARY
ATTRACTION ALERT!

❦

*This rule is gender neutral because anyone who understands enough to see the whole picture can avoid being someone else's pigeon, that is, avoid being taken advantage of. However, there is the male overview, the female overview, and **the** overview that gives each gender a peek into how the other thinks and that we leave to the gods of irony and comedy. Male and female overviews will never be one hundred percent congruent, but, still, a man with an overview, even if it's "just" the male overview, is far more attractive to women than a man who is clueless.*

RULE FOR LIFE #5

INITIATE OR RESPOND CALMLY

We live in an Age of Rage — road rage, sports rage, standing-in-line rage, bicycle rage, and just general, unfocused *"You-lookin'-at-me, what's-your-problem, I'll-kick-your-ass"* rage. If you can buck this trend and complain to someone in a friendly *"Yeah-I-know-stuff-happens,and everything-takes-a cer-tain-amount-of-time"* way, you're probably the only one all day who has. The people you're complaining to will probably do what you want them to do just because of the novelty of the situation.

Plus, you just acted like a grownup, so it's highly unlikely that anyone will spit in your food. Rage and rudeness on your part give the re-cipient permission and inclination to be as aggressive as you're being. If the recipient has the power to screw with you, it's a good bet s/he will, just to show you who's really got the power. On the other hand, a calm and reasonable complaint invites a calm and reasonable response. If it doesn't, you can always go crazy later.

Consider this: certain parts of the human brain contain what are called mirror neurons that fire when we do something *and* when we see *someone else* do that same thing. The mirror neurons fire and get us ready to do whatever that other person is doing. That's why yawning, crying, and laughing are so contagious, and that's the reason you should start every complaint with a calm voice and a friendly smile. When you finally get fed up and begin to escalate, notice that the person you're talking to will tend to match your escalation.

Sometimes, though, you have to act against type. When someone is being too emotional to be able to reach an accord and you can't get him to talk without the emotion, an old cop technique is to escalate and push the other guy to the point that he loses his cool. Once he's out of control, you calm down, get reasonable, and go back to being a grown-up, urging him to calm down, too. Suddenly, you're the grown-up and he's acting like a child throwing a tantrum. Most folks will get embarrassed that they didn't do the grown-up thing first and you will have them in a natural one-down position. Now, you can both deal calmly and reasonably, but you're going to win because you're already one up. I learned this by acting like a child in front of a grown-up.

Back in the old days, when Sears and Roebuck was the place to go for dry goods and tools, their policy for handling customer complaints was simple — identify the exact nature of a complaint and give the customer exactly what s/he wants. One autumn when the world was young, I went down to Sears and bought the cheapest leaf rake they had. When I got home, I went out to the front yard, took one swipe at my leaves with the rake and the handle snapped in half. Already stressed about unrelated business issues, and therefore instantly furious, I went back to Sears with the two pieces and confronted the tool-department clerk.

Giving full vent to my anger, I "explained" the situation. He listened and, when I had finished, he calmly asked, *"What do you want?"* Already operating at the top of my rage meter, I said *"You weren't listening,"* and repeated my rant. Again, when I had finished, he calmly asked, *"Sir, what do you want?"* As I started to reiterate my complaint, it occurred to me that he had asked the right question. I stopped and said, *"I want a full refund of the price of this rake to be applied to my purchase of your top-of-the-line leaf rake."* He said, *"Then that's what we'll do"* and performed the exchange on the spot. If I had started at the lowest rage setting instead of the other end of the scale, the result would have been the same, but I wouldn't have seemed like such a jackass (to both of us).

Later, raking my leaves, I realized that if he had refused my request, I would have left myself nowhere to go. It was a lesson learned and, from that day to this, I start my complaints as reasonable requests and rarely have to drag out the big guns. On those few occasions when those guns are required, they're only marginally effective, if for no other reason than that people naturally want to help a nice friendly person, but they get urges to call security and a S.W.A.T. team when dealing with a raging lunatic.

Worse, getting angry means you're giving up your self-control, which is not something a man does lightly. Stay cool and calm, treat anger like ammo, and you'll be much more effective than the jackass who starts out screaming.

Staying in control of your emotions and your behavior when you're angry is work, but nobody said that being a grown-up is easy. But whether it's easy or hard is irrelevant. What is relevant is that your temper is a tool in your intellectual and emotional kit to be hauled out and used when it's the right tool for the job, and, like other tools, it's not something to be misused, overused, or lost.

CAROLYN'S COMMENTARY
ATTRACTION ALERT!

The man who keeps his cool best wins and he wins the fair maiden. Think James Bond, Batman, and Underdog. Real men who can reason a situation to resolution, rather than escalate it, are very attractive. Women like men who can make us feel safe and protected because they maintain control, instead of losing it and exposing us to the chaos of violence.

NEVER MAKE A DECISION
UNTIL YOU ABSOLUTELY HAVE TO

Once you get beyond childhood, life is just one damn decision after another and timing is always a critical factor. Fortunately, figuring out when to make a decision is easy. As counter-intuitive as it seems at first, the rule is: *never make a decision until you absolutely have to!* Take all the time available to make each decision. If the deadline is in June and you make and execute the decision in January, something critical to the decision will either change in the intervening months and you'll look like an idiot, or everything will change and it'll turn out the decision didn't have to be made at all.

If you have time and know what the decision is going to be, fine. Just don't actually finalize it until the last possible moment because, again, the factors you're considering may change enough in the interim to warrant taking a different course.

If you have time but have no idea what your decision will be, do as much research and analysis as you have the stomach for (and as much as you think the issue warrants), think it through critically to figure it out, and consult whatever experts you think you should. Then, put it out of your conscious mind and let the decision marinate in your unconscious for as long as you can. There are two reasons for doing this: one is that, as we just saw, critical factors and the resulting logical calculus may change. The other is that, when you can delay a decision, your unconscious mind (which has perfect access to everything you know, everything you feel, and which never forgets anything, even if "you" do) will process all the known factors and grind on the decision, no matter how complex, against all your experience and knowledge. When you finally get around to looking at it logically, your unconscious mind will serve up a better analysis and more thorough overview of whatever the issue is than your conscious mind alone ever could. If you can't delay a decision, make it boldly, hope for the best, accept the results with grace, and move on.

The worst thing you can do is to be hasty and make a snap decision when you don't have to. Being hasty is not the same thing as being decisive, but it can be the same thing as being stupid because by moving too fast, you can waste options you could have preserved. Then, you not only look like an idiot, but you've acted like one, too.

Never make a decision until you absolutely have to.

DRAMA ALERT!

Following this rule creates a potential source of emotional conflict between men and women. It works for men, but count on it making the women around you crazy because it revolves around one of the most important and fundamental differences in the way men and women think. Women make snap decisions all the time because we are genetically programmed to multi-task, but not to prioritize among those tasks, so all the many things that are going on at once all have the same weight in our minds. We make decisions immediately to clear something — anything — from our plates and move on to something else.

*That makes men crazy because they don't understand that one vital fact: every single thing in a woman's life may not each have equal importance to her, but each does arouse an equal amount of stress and pressure, and each pulls our attention **equally** all the time. Men seem to think women are ditzy because we make decisions this way. We're not, but constantly moving decisions off our plates is vital under these circumstances and that's why we make snap decisions and why we don't understand when you won't.*

Do you want to reduce the drama you get from the woman in your life? Let her know that the decision she's concerned about is pending. That allows it to be taken off her plate, for a little while at least. Telling a woman you are "working on it" will buy you some time and relieve part of her mind. Taking the time to explain to her why the decision shouldn't be made now and telling her when it will be made is a generous thing to do and a real man chooses to be generous, especially if he wants to remain drama-free.

Keep It Simple and Travel Light, But Never Skimp on Ammo

〰

> "MAY YOU LIVE IN INTERESTING TIMES."
> **ANCIENT CHINESE CURSE**

Life in the modern world is certainly interesting and can be entertaining, but, unless you're very careful, the price of playing the game can be a heavy load of complex issues that cause wear and tear on the heart in the form of maximum stress. A heavy load takes the fun out of life and stress kills. The simpler you can keep your life, and the less emotional conflict you agree to deal with, that is, the less drama you participate in, the better your life will be and the more fun you'll have. Ammo in this context refers to the essential tools you use in whatever your trade is or whatever you use to simplify and prevent or remove stress. I'm talking things like cash, reasons, evidence, leverage, and so on. The more of life's challenges you can anticipate, the more acceptable alternate responses you can devise, and the better you get at prioritizing your strategies, the more powder you put in that ammo and the more effective it will be. Of course, this metaphor doesn't refer to bullets and grenades unless, of course, you're in an actual combat zone.

Therefore, this rule has a physical application as well as an emotional one.

On the physical side, one of Murphy's more insidious laws is that no matter what you set out to do, invariably something else must be done first. In other words, although they say a journey of a thousand miles begins with a single step, what it really starts with is having to go find an ATM to get some cash and swinging by the cleaner's to pick up your laundry. Each element, step, or moving part in your plan or system is a potential point of failure, delay, or bifurcation, so the fewer of them there are, the less likely it is that something will fail or go wrong or divert you from your original purpose. More importantly, you'll have fewer things to remember and the older you get, the more important that becomes. So, keeping it simple is good.

The lighter you travel, the more agile you can be. In this case, agility means the ability to respond to changing conditions quickly and easily without being weighed down by extra stuff. Picture a man carrying a small rucksack and that same man carrying a footlocker. So, traveling light means resisting the tyranny of your possessions and taking only those things you absolutely need, but it doesn't mean skimping on ammo.

The emotional application of this rule is a bit murkier because it operates in those deep, confusing levels much closer to the psychological and emotional bone. Keeping it simple and traveling light emotionally does not mean that you shouldn't feel or foster deep emotions, and it certainly doesn't mean that you should limit the number of people you care deeply about.

Instead, it refers to limiting the amount of drama you're willing to accept in the day-to-day conduct of your emotional life, because drama can be a very heavy load. Life being what it is, there will inevitably be moments when the flap count (picture a hen house both with and without the fox — the difference is the flap count) on the Drama-tron just naturally redlines. At that point, you're stuck with having to brave heavy emotional gravity storms to resolve whatever the issue is. But times like that should be the rare exception rather than the rule. If it begins to happen too often, consider simplifying your life and lightening your load.

You can simplify by lighting a shuck for parts unknown or by going fishing for long enough to start to breathe again. You can also lighten your load by removing the source of all the drama from your life, no matter what that source is, and once again keeping it simple and traveling light.

CAROLYN'S COMMENTARY

            ❧

Males hate drama. What they don't understand is that there are levels of drama. The first level is pure frustration. The second comes from generalized, unfocused fears. The third arises when we are just pissed off. The challenge is that, much of the time, we women can't even tell the difference. But no matter why it happens, when a woman turns into a Drama Queen, there is a significant risk that the men around her will shut down and wait for her to stop, or will shut down and simply walk away.

 Ladies, understand that clearly. A man may stay with you in spite of the drama, but he won't stay with you because of it and you won't get what you want until the drama ends. Therefore, either don't start it in the first place — which is best — or if you're really addicted to high-risk behavior, watch his reaction and as soon as the "power button" shuts down and he's ready to walk away (or the hammer is cocked and he's ready to turn and fight), it's time to shut up, smile, breathe, and wait. When you end the drama, the right response has the best chance of appearing. It'll appear far sooner if you never start, because men hate drama.

RULE FOR LIFE #8

QUESTION EVERYTHING

⁓⊗⁓

A man is responsible for his actions. When other people are depending on him to make good decisions, he needs to be as certain as he can be that the information he's acting on is reliable and the conclusions he's drawing from that information are reasonable. Fine, but the world is full of more than just misinformation, disinformation, mendacity, spin, and opinion. It's also full of conflicting evidence, deep complexity, inaccurate translations, fantasy, hope, wishful thinking, delusion, and, worst of all, nonlinearity. Of all of these sources of inaccuracy, nonlinearity is the most insidious because it confounds our expectations, like a good cutting horse throws an inexperienced rider. Neither the universe nor the horse are acting with malice, but nonetheless, suddenly there you are, lying in a clump of brush wondering *"What just happened?"* and *"Which way did they go?"*

A man has to question everything.

Nothing happens unless it's caused by something else and it's rarely caused by just one or two things. Usually, something is caused by a long chain of interrelated causes. That chain of causality is impossibly complex because of the sheer size of it all. When anything in the universe happens, it affects everything else to some degree because everything is interconnected. Sometimes that effect is minuscule, occurring in a distant galaxy and we here on Earth never notice. Sometimes the effect is local and vast.

But wait. It's not even that simple. There are an infinite number of such causal chains at work at any given time, contributing an infinite number of factors and elements with strange laws governing their interoperation. That immense complexity completely defeats the internal logic of the human mind and causes the universe to appear to be completely random and disturbingly non-linear. So, if the universe acts random-and-non-linear, it might as well be random-and-non-linear, right?

The scientific community, with its gift for poetry, says that nature's processes are "computationally irreducible phenomena." In English that means that there's just no way to tell what's going to happen next until after it's already happened. You and I know that computationally irreducible phenomena are not really random, but the appearance of randomness they present will certainly suffice until real randomness shows up. Either way, being certain of anything under such nonlinear circumstances is highly problematic.

If the world were simple and linear, you could operate by deductive reasoning and be as certain of your conclusions as Sherlock Holmes. In a non-linear world, however, only an idiot is absolutely certain of *anything*, because non-linearity is full of illusions and leaps and discontinuities, sudden shifts and sharp turns and shades of gray. Doesn't that sound like your life yesterday and the day before and last month and last year?

So, you do your research and you get by with a little help from your friends by asking them for their opinions. As soon as you do, you get parallax views and that can be very helpful. Parallax is the apparent change in the position of something when it is viewed along two different lines of sight, like when you close one eye and sight down the edge of a ruler and then close that eye and open the other one. It appears to the new eye as if the ruler had moved. Your eyes are a couple of inches apart, so they see things from different perspectives. Friends and counselors also see things from different perspectives, so their opinions may show you something you hadn't seen ... or they may just confirm your own suspicions. Either way, parallax opinions are helpful.

One more time, just to make sure we've all got it: the mismatch between the way the world is (complex and non-linear) and the way we think it should work (simply and logically) arises from the fact that the universe follows such complex laws and has such multi-faceted interactions that we can't even begin to follow its own internal logic. In fact, we still don't even know all the terms and facts and forces that feed into that logic.

Our thinking, on the other hand, is a product of our physical bodies whose day-to-day experience seems to confirm, rightly or wrongly, the results of simple cause and effect and tends to misdiagnose randomness by being adept at noticing patterns that aren't really there, like seeing faces in the clouds and virgins on tortillas. The problem with that is that absolute randomness contains strings of events that appear to have pattern. But, since those apparent patterns may or may not be meaningful, there's no way to know just what it is that you don't know.

Here's why: mathematicians have shown that if you could flip a coin $10^{1,000,0007}$ times*, (that's a ten followed by one million and seven zeros, a very large number) there would be at least 10 strings of 1 million heads (or tails) in a row. If you get bored and stop flipping after only 100,000 (10^4, a ten followed by four zeros) trials or a million (10^5, a ten followed by five zeros) trials, you could be inside one of those strings and just not know it. You could therefore reasonably and logically assume that every time you flipped a coin, it would come up heads. That's an entirely logical and reasonable conclusion based on that particular set of observed facts, but we all know that it just isn't true. The next time you flip a coin, you could be inside an entirely different string of random results.

Therefore, you can never be absolutely certain of your conclusions, because, as we've just shown, non-linearity precludes certainty. What you can do when you make a plan is to do your best, make contingency plans, stay loose, keep alert, be ready, stay balanced on the perceptive balls of your mental feet, wait for events to ricochet, assume nothing, question everything, and always keep an eye out for the nearest deep cover.

---

*Writing that number out in a Times Roman size 10 font on regular copy paper, using one inch margins all around, would take a 10 followed by 289 pages of zeros.

CAROLYN'S COMMENTARY
ATTRACTION ALERT!

For a woman, certainty is a very attractive quality, but so are flexibility and a willingness to adapt. If nothing is certain in our world, women love it when you face an uncertain situation by making a decision and a plan. We like it even more when you fill us in during the planning process and we like it best of all when you consult us as well. Who knows, we may even have a piece of crucial information that may help tweak the plan. If it doesn't work, admitting you were wrong, if and when you are wrong, gets you big points. At that point, blaming it on the randomness of the world is just fine with us.

ALWAYS HAVE
A CONTINGENCY PLAN

～≈～

You always need to plan your actions, even if it's just a quick *"I'll do that first 'cause it's on the way, I'll do that when I get there, and I'll do this on the way back because it could run into extra innings."* In more serious planning, Plan A is your best guess at how to get what you want most effectively. But, remember that Rule #8 says that non-linearity precludes certainty. So, you devise a contingency Plan B, which is an alternate route, just in case. Then, the world being as typically uncooperative as it is, you devise Plan C, which is a fall-back position.

You get to thinking about it and go get Plan D, which is a flask of good whiskey because, well, you just never know and it helps to be prepared. Then you get to thinking about Plan E, which is the way you can change events and circumstances enough to make your original plan (Plan A) work.

You formulate Plan F in case nothing else works out because it sounds an awful lot like *"Make a run for the border and live quietly in an undisclosed tropical location under an assumed name until the statute of limitations runs out back home,"* and the mental image of quiet safety can be comforting.

But, no matter what your plan is, always think through the contingency plans so, instead of being caught leaning or worse, being caught flatfooted, you'll be as prepared as you can be for whatever happens next.

CAROLYN'S COMMENTARY
ATTRACTION ALERT!

Women like men who are prepared for whatever happens, even if it's unexpected. However, if a female is involved in — or affected by — the plan and you share the planning with her, you may be surprised at her input and she may even have been there already and know a shortcut. Women like to be consulted and are attracted to men who show enough respect to include us in the contingency-planning process.

RULE FOR LIFE #10

NOTHING IN LIFE IS FREE, SO ALWAYS IDENTIFY THE COST

You can only do one thing at a time, so, when you choose to do that one thing, you're also choosing not to do something else. The short-term cost of doing what you do is not being able to do some other thing. If you go fishing, you can't play golf at the same time.

Of course, there may be additional mid-term costs involved as well. For instance, if you know going fishing will make you late for dinner and you stop just long enough to make a phone call and let someone know, the cost of doing it is the small amount of time that action takes you. The cost of not doing it may be a cold dinner, a cold shoulder, and a day of hurt feelings by someone you love. Understanding the cost of your actions is important — cold spaghetti is bad enough, but cold spaghetti and a cold shoulder are awful, especially when both are avoidable.

Some costs are long-term. The whole issue of recreational drugs makes this point clearly. The reason that recreational drug-use is such a vast problem is that, in the very beginning when the real cost is unclear, recreational drug use can seem like a lot of fun and, if you're an idiot, can seem very cool. But, remember, the drug dealer's credo is *"I got something for you, but you only get the first one free."* The drug dealer knows that the true cost of doing drugs is always paid on the back end, and that you're going to give him money every single day until you pay the final price. If he knows it, you should, too. When a man hears, *"Hey, buddy. You gotta try this,"* he's got to be able to assess the true cost of trying it.

Indiscriminate sex is a lot like a recreational drug. It's huge fun, addictive, and warps your perspective so much that it can be very difficult to assess the true cost of your actions until it's way too late. But, even if you don't have to deal with inadvertent paternity, incurable disease, imminent death, a crippled self-image, or just a 12-week course of antibiotics, you may still have to be nice to someone you've discovered you'd really rather not hang out with.

Everything has a cost and, since it's the hidden costs that can be the most oppressive and expensive — which is exactly why they're hidden — you'd damn well better know, or, at least think about, what they are.

One of the subtler aspects of this rule is that you not only have to know the cost of what you do or acquire, but you also have to understand the cost of maintaining what you already have. That is, are you suffering under the tyranny of your possessions or your relationships? Owning a house is a good thing, but it makes it much harder to pull up stakes and move to another city, especially in a down real estate market. Having children launches your genes and name into the future, but makes it tougher for you and your wife to slip off to the islands on the spur of the moment. Owning a sexy Italian sports car may impress the girls, but it makes four-wheeling to fish remote lakes impossible. Getting married almost always puts a significant crimp in your dating life.

In short, everything has a cost. Knowing what that cost is makes deciding if you can afford it, or if you even really want it, easier.

CAROLYN'S COMMENTARY
ATTRACTION ALERT!

A woman's first reaction to this rule is, "Duh!" because we do most of the shopping and because we know intimately that our actions have consequences. An evening of romance can lead to an afternoon of childbirth. An engaging chat on the cell phone can lead to bent fenders. Everything has a cost and, as women who have to carry the burden of bearing children and, occasionally, carrying groceries, this is an accepted fact of life. A man who understands the consequences of his actions before he acts and accepts them afterwards is very attractive to women because such behavior shows both maturity and integrity.

FEEL THE FEAR
BUT ACT WITH COURAGE

This rule is really about fear and risk and how a man deals with them. Some people will tell you that *"A real man is fearless."* No, only an idiot is fearless. Scary stuff scares a man because he's just a human being, but also because a man always pays attention and understands why he should be afraid of something. He just doesn't let that fear rule his behavior.

Sometimes the scary stuff can be lethal, like unarmed hand-to-hand combat with an angry grizzly bear protecting her cub, or running into a burning building to save a child. Anybody who says he's not afraid of things like that is lying.

Sometimes the scary stuff is merely serious, like trying dances you don't really know how to do in public or the 30 minutes just after your intimate other says *"We have to talk."* Either way, making mistakes is a part of life, so just cowboy up, do the best you can, and show a little courage.

The dictionary defines courage as facing extreme danger without fear. Nonsense. Courage is being scared out of your wits, frightened to death, absolutely certain you're going to get drawn and quartered and that it's going to hurt a lot, but doing what has to be done anyhow. Any idiot can do something he's not afraid of doing. Having courage is feeling the fear, but acting boldly in spite of it.

In day-to-day life, however, you'll very rarely be asked to charge a machine gun nest with just a knife in your teeth or wrestle a grizzly bear without even the knife. More often, you'll find yourself faced with a situation in which you really don't want to make a mistake because it'll be embarrassing, or you'll look bad, or people will think you're a dork, or some other reasonable concern.

Get over it, because mistakes are an unavoidable part of life, they can be valuable learning experiences, and most of the time they won't kill you. Feel the fear, but don't let it stop you from acting boldly and doing what has to be done.

CAROLYN'S COMMENTARY
ATTRACTION ALERT!

If "losing face" in your culture is fatal, then avoid "losing face." However, if embarrassment or mistakes could lead to some sort of breakthrough or experience, cowboy up, take your turn, and take your licks. Women admire boldness and courage.

RULE FOR LIFE #12

SET HIGH STANDARDS. MARGINAL PERFORMANCE IS UNACCEPTABLE

No matter what a man sets out to do, he must do his best. His best may not be very good, but if it's his best, if he gives it his all, that's all that really matters ... most of the time. There's an element of integrity about doing your best in everything. The choir may not ask you to sing, but if they do, no one can ask more of someone than that he gives his best effort.

Sometimes it doesn't make much difference. If you and a buddy are in a pick-up basketball game for bragging rights, give it your best, have some fun, and don't sweat the small stuff. Sometimes it will make a lot of difference. If you and a buddy are challenged to a pool game by a couple of slicks for a hundred dollars a ball and you aren't very good, you might want to make certain your buddy understands that before he has a chance to get in too deep.

An agreement to perform at something is just that. It's an agreement, also known as a contract, and a man honors his contracts. If the choir leader belongs to the joyful-noise contingent and says she doesn't care if you can carry a tune (and if you're certain she means it), then go have a good time. Just be certain that your personal integrity ensures that you do your best and don't agree to provide more than your best is capable of delivering.

Once you're doing your best, you have the right to expect it of others, so if you never slack off yourself, you never have to accept anything but a true best-effort from those people you're depending on. If everybody's doing their best, one of the really pleasant facts you discover pretty quickly is that people (yourself included) have phenomenal capacity and you can accomplish damn near anything you set your mind to.

CAROLYN'S COMMENTARY
ATTRACTION ALERT!

❦

Yup. Women really like a man who always does his best.

STOP AND CORRECT SCREW-UPS BEFORE CONTINUING

~~✦~~

Everyone makes mistakes. How you respond when your turn comes will make a huge difference in your life. When you make a mistake or when you see things starting to ricochet out of control, stop what you're doing and correct the problem if you can.

If you try to correct it on the fly, there's a pretty good chance you'll just make things worse, because, the way we're wired, we are unable to think deeply as we go. We must *stop* to think. So, stop. Fix it. Then move on.

Often, things seem to go well until one thing goes wrong. Then there is an avalanche of events that sends everything off in all directions. At times like this it would be easy to believe that the whole world is waiting for the proverbial straw to fall at just the right point of stress so all hell can break loose ... and, you'd be right. It is.

Of course, there are single errors whose magnitude increases across time or distance. Chaos Theory calls the effects of these single errors "sensitive dependence on initial conditions," or, "the Butterfly Effect." A good

example of sensitive dependence on initial conditions is a one degree aim-
ing error at the barrel of a rifle. If your aim is off just one degree, you'll
miss a target 50 yards away by about 31 inches. At 100 yards, you'll miss
by just over five feet. At a 1,000 yards, you'll miss by nearly 17 yards. At
5,000 yards, you'll miss by a nearly a whole football field.

There are other times in which the exact moment whatever system
you're dealing with starts spinning out of control will remain unde-
tectable. It doesn't seem to make any difference whether the system is a
physical system like tectonic structures miles below the earth's surface,
an organizational system like a political structure or a stock market, or
an emotional system like a human being's coping structure. Collapse
comes as a surprise.

Stress on any stable portion of the system won't necessarily cause
an issue, but stress on a portion riddled with instability can cause system-
wide domino-effect catastrophes like earthquakes or stock market
crashes. Things go wrong in bunches, because the stability of the whole
system is contingent on the inter-related stabilities of each tiny part. One
tiny event in the wrong place can cause several more which cause several
more each which ... well, you get the idea.

But that doesn't mean you're not going to get blamed when everything goes south. You are. After all, you were the one making things happen. Who else's fault could it possibly be? Accept that, rise above it, or get
past it any way you can, and your life will be simpler and easier to get
through. Fight it, and you're going to be very unhappy, dealing with unhappy folks who can't understand why you just can't quite get it right.
Accept the blame cheerfully and they'll judge from your calm acceptance

that you've got it all under control. Believe it or not, your own equanimity will make all the difference.

Therefore, when a chain of catastrophic events starts, ride it out if you can, as best you can, and when it finally stops (that is, when the system stabilizes again), you stop, too. Breathe. Figure out what happened or why you're making mistakes, correct them if you can, adjust to the new situation, get back in the saddle, and move on.

CAROLYN'S COMMENTARY
DRAMA ALERT!

Everyone makes mistakes, but few things are more attractive to a woman than a man who is accountable for his actions or results (good or bad), and who is willing to do what it takes to fix it and make it work. When a man says "I've got it" and means it, we (women) can relax, as long as he has let us in on the plan. We can be really supportive if we are clear on what we are supporting and why we should. But, if we see trouble looming and we don't know how you plan to deal with it, or what is going on, look out, because the drama is about to hit the fan.

Drama is a good indicator that we sense danger or feel insecure. We may also resort to nagging. Sorry about that, but the information we need to calm our instincts is knowing there is a plan. Nagging is the tool we use to gain that knowledge. It's just our way and we do it because it works. Clarity is power. A man who recognizes his mistakes, stops and fixes them, and keeps his woman clearly informed in the process will have a much better relationship with her than a guy who doesn't.

RULE FOR LIFE #14

IF YOU HAVE TO THROW A PUNCH, YOU'VE FAILED AND SHOULD BE ASHAMED

Grownups don't get into fights, but they do defend themselves. Getting into a fight isn't manly. It's criminal — either a misdemeanor or a felony, depending on the details. Sure, there are times when we'd all like to give someone a richly deserved spanking, beat the crap out of someone who has it coming, or step in and kick someone's ass because they've asked for it. The legal term for doing so is "assault" and the term for the result can be "incarceration." The term for dissuading someone from throwing a punch in the first place is "being a grown-up." The term for defending yourself from a physical attack is "self-defense." The term for not knowing the difference is "stupid."

It's okay to be salty. It's okay to be assertive. It's also okay to be smart enough to defuse the situation when someone else wants to fight, because if you allow somebody dumber than you are to take control of the situation away from you, to quote the song, *"Somebody's going to emer-*

*gency; somebody's going to jail."** Neither is necessary. Both are aggressively stupid, but maybe you can use the 30 days you'll spend sitting in a county cell to think through the error of your ways.

What it boils down to is that a gentleman should be able to protect himself and others and to handle himself in a throw-down, but he should also be smart enough to control the situation well enough to avoid violence.

CAROLYN'S COMMENTARY

❧

*Women, at least grown-up women, don't fight as a general rule. We may scream, cry, and throw things, but physical violence is not generally our first — or last — reaction. So the fighting and going to jail thing makes little sense to most of us. But if you are fighting for **our** honor, well, my heavens, throwing a punch or two is so gallant. But stupid, and women have trouble getting excited about stupid men. Walk away secure in the knowledge that there will be something else to fight about tomorrow, but at least you can confront it with a woman on your arm instead of on your case.*

---

*From the Don Henley song "New York Minute," from the album *The End of the Innocence.*

Power Through Unpleasant Tasks Without Whining

Sometimes a man has no choice but to face an unpleasant, dangerous, or repugnant task — but one that has to be done. When you realize you're faced with something that is inevitable and requires action, don't hesitate and don't complain. Just power through whatever it is, get it done to the best of your ability, and — if you survive — move on.

CAROLYN'S COMMENTARY
ATTRACTION ALERT!

❧

This rule is universal. I was told once by a man, a client I respect, "Suck it up, princess, and get 'er done." Women admire men who are decisive, who face up to what has to be done, and who fulfill their responsibilities.

WHAT CANNOT BE CHANGED
MUST BE BORNE

❧

"ANY IDIOT CAN FACE A CRISIS; IT'S JUST
THIS DAY-TO-DAY LIVING THAT WEARS YOU OUT."
ANTON CHEKOV

A man has to learn to walk on shaky ground and swim in muddy waters because most of the things that will happen in his life will be completely beyond his control. That fact causes problems precisely because the issue of control is central to the human psyche.

In fact, when a person — man or woman — feels out of control or experiences a defeat of some sort, it is such a powerful psychic event that the emotions engendered by it actually trigger a physical glandular response in the body. Long ago, this syndrome was called "dying of a broken heart," because, if the loss of control or feeling of defeat is serious or prolonged enough, the physical deterioration can lead to disease and death.

However, when that same person wins or otherwise gains the illusion of control, the immune and limbic systems light up, activity in the hypothalamus ratchets up a notch or two, and the system is flooded with testosterone. As a result, he feels elation and a surge in both confidence and aggression. Of course, as any honky-tonk jukebox will tell you, too much testosterone can cause too much confidence to be mixed with too much aggression and the results can also kill a person.

That being true, it is unsettling to realize that control is always an illusion. The constant advancing flow of mathematics, small-particle and quantum physics, chaos, complexity, synchrony theory, ubiquity theory, and the socio-biological and cognitive sciences show that the world is an infinitely complex and effectively random environment. But, in the short run, we do get the comforting, stimulating, and very real *illusion* of control and, in this, as in so many other things, it is our illusions that sustain us.

So, even if you can't control events, you can control your responses to them and some control is better than none at all.

If you can resolve an issue or do something about a problem (that is, control it), do it. If not, control your own thoughts so you don't just sit and cry, wallow in your lack of control, and waste time by worrying. You control your thoughts by shoving whatever issue you're confronting down into your unconscious. Your unconscious will then do what it does best: it will grind on the problem at levels far below your awareness and will likely come up with a solution, or, at least, an acceptable response. Too much conscious thought inhibits that process. In fact, cognition scientists are now saying the unconscious is where the majority of our decision-making is actually done.

But, whether you solve the problem or not, you still have to be able to discharge your responsibilities with confidence and take care of business with courage, and you can't do that if you're distracted by fretting. When things are hard, it can be difficult to keep enough perspective to maintain a positive attitude. But, you can keep most of the dark periods at bay by cultivating a habitual mental toughness.

You have to learn to slip the punches life will throw at you, absorb the ones you can't slip, and maintain a positive-enough attitude to perform effectively. Physically tough people learn to bear the stress, accept the pain, and control their physical reactions. Mentally tough people learn to accept the stress, contain the pain, and control their thoughts.

Controlling your thoughts takes effort, and the first step is to understand that nothing is ever as bad — or as good — as you thought it was going to be. Real life is an essentially messy business and catastrophe is a natural part of it. Your natural tendency when a catastrophe hits is to panic, but it's also precisely the time you need to be calm and under control. Expect disaster, prepare for it mentally, and when it hits, weather it calmly without taking it personally. When it's over, you can fall apart if you really need to, but go somewhere private first. There's no need to shake people's confidence in you unnecessarily.

Drowning kittens.

To understand just how hard controlling your thoughts is, don't allow yourself to think about drowning kittens for the next two weeks. If the thought of drowning kittens comes into your mind, stop the thought immediately and replace that thought with a different one. Now, don't let the thoughts of kittens slowly drowning in a tied-up sack return.

It's hard, isn't it?

It's an important skill to develop, though. There are certain thoughts you can't afford to think at certain times because they will drain away the emotional energy you need to perform important tasks, or, just as bad, they'll distract you. Either way, those tasks won't get done. Not thinking of certain things at specific times is called compartmentalization. In the beginning, it's hard to do, but so are 200 push-ups the first time you try. Compartmentalization works when you refuse to allow a thought to occupy your conscious mind. You consciously stop thinking it, push it down, and immediately think of something else. As we've just discussed, there are very good reasons to become adept at compartmentalization.

To recap, when there is truly nothing you can do about an issue or coming event except worry about it or contemplate it in horror, you waste mental effort and physical time by thinking about it. Worse, if you concentrate on thoughts of defeat or fear, your body will drain away the strength and resolve you need just when you need them most and invite fatigue, despair, and illness.

The key to bearing what cannot be changed is achieving enough mental toughness to compartmentalize your thoughts sufficiently to clear the conscious mind. This frees it to work on issues it can handle, putting your unconscious mind to work on the really gnarly issues facing you. Most of the time, mental toughness will give you the internal tools to bear whatever must be borne.

CAROLYN'S COMMENTARY
DRAMA ALERT!

❧

Drowning kittens. Really? Was there more to this rule? Oh, yes, compartmentalization. Compartmentalization is a purely masculine discipline because women multi-task instead. Multi-tasking (the natural way women have evolved to operate) is the exact opposite of compartmentalization (the natural way men have evolved to operate). When women understand that men can and should compartmentalize to be brilliant at what they do in any given moment, that understanding may allow a greater peace to reign between the sexes. Unless you've had a long talk with her about the whole issue of compartmentalization and mental toughness, the woman has no idea why it's important to you and will think you're just being irritatingly male and possibly lazy to boot. If the woman is important enough to you, get this issue on the table and get to an understanding. It may protect you from a lot of drama.

RULES FOR HAVING FUN

RULE FOR HAVING FUN #1

A MAN ALWAYS
REMAINS A GENTLEMAN

A real man makes a conscious decision to be a gentleman, but that doesn't mean he's weak. In fact, not so long ago calling a gentleman a weakling (or a liar or a coward or any other term that indicated a lack of respect) would get you struck across the face and challenged to a duel. Such a gentleman who survived one or more such encounters was called a "killing gentleman," that is, a gentleman with a hard streak who wouldn't hesitate a whit to kill you in defense of his honor or on behalf of a woman's honor or for any other reason he deemed sufficient.

Fortunately, those days are gone (outside of some cowboy, shrimper, or biker bars), but you still can't assume that just because a man is a gentleman you can be rude and get out of an encounter unscathed. A gentleman is still a man. A hundred years ago being a gentleman meant you had money and probably owned land. Today it often refers to a man who has manners and a strong sense of personal honor, who shows gallantry and chivalry toward women and who thinks for himself.

In short, a gentleman is a gentle man who lives by an honorable code and treats others with respect — at least, he does until they demonstrate by their own behavior that they are willing to forfeit any claim to respect and the protections it affords. Once people demonstrate by bad behavior that they have willingly forfeited their right to be respected, all bets are off.

A number of years ago, I was in a grocery store to pick up a few things for my wife. As I pushed my basket down one long aisle, I saw there were two women standing beside each other talking, with their carts side-by-side facing in opposite directions and completely blocking the passage. I could see the item I needed just beyond them, but I couldn't get to it. I just stood there waiting for them to move. Finally, after a minute or so, I cleared my throat and said *"Excuse me,"* thinking that maybe they just hadn't noticed that I was trying to get past them. They both looked at me with a touch of imperious hostility, then went back to their conversation without any other acknowledgment and certainly without moving aside. Okay, now that's just rude, so I smiled and said, *"Ladies, that's my fault. I said that in English. I'll translate it into American for you: 'GET THE HELL OUT OF THE WAY!'"* They both scurried aside and, as I pushed my cart through, I, a gentleman once again, smiled sweetly and said, *"Thank you, ladies."*

Courtesy earns courtesy and rudeness begets rudeness. A man who lives by the code outlined in this book will be, by default, a gentleman right up to the point at which he makes the conscious decision not to be.

CAROLYN'S COMMENTARY

ATTRACTION ALERT!

❧

Women know gentlemen when we see them or better yet when we are in their presence and, yes, we like that. Unfortunately, we live in a society where women were forced to take on masculine attributes in the work place and sometimes mistook gentlemanly behavior for condescension, ("Hey, pal, I can open my own door.") Women had few female role models to follow into the work place, so we followed the more aggressive male model. Hopefully, that model has now changed so that women can go back to being strong and powerful without having to act like men, but, better, so men can go back to acting like gentlemen, because women really, really like being around men who are gentlemen.

ALWAYS REACH CONTENTMENT LONG BEFORE CAPACITY AND RETAIN ENOUGH SELF-CONTROL TO HELP THE FALLEN

~

"AN ETHICAL ANGLER DOES MORE THAN WHAT IS REQUIRED, AND LESS THAN WHAT IS ALLOWED."

AS QUOTED FROM AN OLD FISHING REGULATIONS BOOKLET FROM ALBERTA, BRITISH COLUMBIA, BY JOHN GIERACH IN *FOOL'S PARADISE.*

The stronger a man is, the more dangerous he becomes and the more physical and psychic damage he can do (to himself and others) when he gets out of control. If a man's function is to care for and protect his loved ones or others in his tribe, and his ethics won't allow him to hurt strangers unnecessarily, he can't allow himself to get out of control. It's a matter of integrity, pride, and duty.

Therefore, this rule is about making it a general habit to take pride in remaining in control of yourself by understanding your capacities. Stop before you reach the limits of that capacity and be content with stopping.

This refers primarily to the issue of drinking alcohol and has appeared on signs over the bars in a number of fine eating and drinking establishments on both sides of the Atlantic. When a guy is still a boy, usually a teenager, he experiments with his limits and capacities. That's why getting drunk to the point of passing out in a pool of your own vomit or of throwing up all over a date's shoes is called "getting high-schooled." Dealing with the shame and other consequences of such actions seems to be a rite of passage in a guy's early years.

But a man learns quickly to achieve contentment long before capacity. Then he learns that its true value is that it can be extended and extrapolated to apply to all sorts of other areas, including things like chasing women, eating sweets, buying fly rods, and using credit. A man should apologize easily when necessary, but shouldn't get himself into a situation that he has to apologize for very often.

CAROLYN'S COMMENTARY

ATTRACTION ALERT!

❦

When a man has exceeded his capacity and is out of control, it becomes scary and dangerous. It also becomes the cause of some of the most common and intense disagreements between men and women. Women expect men to know when to stop anything that could be harmful and to know better than to lose the ability to judge. On an instinctual level, women are always afraid of the "tiger" and when the male in question loses control and the ability to protect us from the "tiger," which is your job, you become the "tiger." We hate being around a guy who is out of control, so a man who retains control and can make us feel safe is very attractive.

CAPACITY IS A MOVING TARGET
SO A MAN ALWAYS KEEPS
HIS ANTENNAE UP

This rule is very closely related to the previous one, but they are just different enough to warrant being discussed separately. The previous rule is about *planning* to reach contentment and stopping when you reach it. This rule says that, because ambient conditions change constantly and therefore a man's capacity for anything is always a moving target, he has to stay aware and constantly *adjust* his stopping point in order to be able to fulfill his responsibilities.

For instance, the net effect of a large whiskey after a full meal in a beach house at sea level on Perdido Key on the Redneck Riviera of Alabama is radically different on an empty stomach at 9,000 feet in a mountain cabin in Monument Gulch, Colorado.

In fact, a man always stays aware of his situation and his surroundings and keeps his antennae up, partially so he doesn't exceed his capacity for almost anything: alcohol, pain, drama, driving, exercise, fishing, money, sex, intrigue, arguments with insurance companies, and so on. In fact, the only two things I can think of I could never have more of than I could handle are laughter and love. For everything else, a man pays close attention to current conditions and adjusts his estimations of capacity accordingly.

CAROLYN'S COMMENTARY
ATTRACTION ALERT!

A man who understands his limits and that they change from situation to situation and still can handle himself with control is very attractive, both because a woman feels safe with such a man and because it saves us from unknowingly overstepping, making a mistake, and walking into a tirade that has little to do with us. Getting along is hard enough when we're both in control. A man who stays in control will likely have a good time with a woman and bring out the best in her.

·Practice All Things in Moderation, Especially Moderation

Although this rule seems to provide the exception to the last two, a man still honors his responsibilities and remains a gentleman at all times, even when he's howling at the moon and peeing off the porch. Taking things in moderation is a lot like reaching contentment before capacity. The problem is this. There's no such thing as too much, but there are many times when there is more than you can handle. Making a habit of moderation can help avoid those times. But, I also subscribe to the Confucian belief that just as there is no good without evil, no beauty without ugliness, no success without failure, and no up without down, there is no yin of reasonable moderation without the yang of unreasonable excess.

I firmly believe that, every once in a great while, you have to cut your wolf loose and raise some serious, teetering-on-the-brink-of-total-catastrophe hell. We're talking two-weeks-in-a-strange-town-under-an-assumed-name hell-raising. I am not saying that you should wake up in a hotel room with freshly inked, vastly obscene tattoos and no memory of the past week. But I am saying that occasionally you should howl at the moon and stomp on the terra just to confirm that you're still alive. Just make sure that you don't impinge on the rights of others, you remain a gentleman, you carry enough cash to make your own bail (or better yet, leave it with a friend you can call), and that you're prepared to accept the full consequences of your actions. Finally, make sure that when you're finished living it up, you can live it all down again within the time it takes to cure the inevitable rash.

CAROLYN'S COMMENTARY
DRAMA ALERT!

Few women really understand that men need to do this occasionally. Therefore, if you're going to howl at the moon, either provide advance notice to the women you care about or actually go to a strange town under an assumed name before you start. Otherwise, expect trouble.

RULE FOR HAVING FUN #5

CULTIVATE YOUR ABILITY TO FIND HIDDEN BEAUTY

Not all beauty can be captured by a camera in much the same way a book's cover doesn't really tell you much about what's inside. Some beauty will be hidden quite cunningly, but the better you get at finding that hidden beauty, the richer your life will be. I've met ugly men and homely women who talked themselves beautiful quickly, and I've met beautiful men and women who talked themselves ugly in less than a paragraph.

We've all had the experience in which we see a stranger and notice odd things about the way he looks until we've known him for a while, at which point, we can't see that person we originally saw any more. Instead of that odd-looking person, we see our friend Joe and that ominous squint in the stranger's eyes has been replaced by the sweet laugh lines around our friend's eyes.

On the other hand, sometimes you see a beautiful girl walk into the room and talk with her for a couple of minutes. You either find out she's been the third-runner-up in the Miss Home-Wrecker Pageant four years in a row and won the Western Regional Plastic-Surgery-Enhanced Pout-Offs for the last six, or she bores you into a coma, or, hallelujah, you find that she's smart, sweet, and funny — the fun-evening trifecta.

However, there are all kinds of beauty in this world and not all of it will walk up and slap you across the face to get you to notice it. A vista of mountains with snowy peaks may take your breath away when you encounter it, but the beauty of first light in the high desert may be much more subtle and require that you bring more to the perceptual table than just an ability to be overwhelmed.

Beauty's appearance is sometimes anything but flashy. In the 1990's, I went to one of my favorite restaurants in Los Angeles seeking dinner. I'd never had trouble getting a table there before, but as I walked in the door, the proprietress came running up and apologized, saying that there was an Armenian birthday party going on, the place was full to bursting, and that she wouldn't be able to seat me for a couple of hours, at best. Life is like that sometimes, so as I stood in the foyer trying to de-cide what to do in the alternative, she came up behind me and said, *"The two ladies at the table by the fountain would like to have you join them."* I agreed immediately and thanked her. When I got to the table, I found that one of the ladies was eighty years old and the other was seventy-nine. I smiled and, as I sat down, thanked them for their generosity and hospitality. I ex-pected a knitting-needles-and-tales-of-the-grandson evening, but during the ensuing conversation, it came out that the eighty-year-old had been a Ziegfeld Girl in Vaudeville and the seventy-nine-year-old had been a star-let in the old Hollywood studio system. Those two buzz saws were a pair to draw to, full of life, full of hell, and as charming and enthralling as any women I've ever met, before or since. I had a great time, but the best parts were that I got to call my wife in Denver the next morning and tell her I'd been picked up the night before by a couple of show girls. Then, every time I went back to L.A., I'd call these two and the three of us would go out to dinner. They were beautiful in every way that matters, huge fun to boot, and kept me rapt night after night with tales of a world I've read about but which disappeared long before I finally stumbled into puberty.

When you get a chance to look beneath surface appearances or the most obvious details and find what's really there, you can wind up living in a more beautiful world than other people do. We can all recognize ugliness when it shows itself, but a man who pays close enough attention will find the hidden beauty.

CAROLYN'S COMMENTARY
ATTRACTION ALERT!

❧

*I think this may be my favorite of all these rules. It gives all women —
those of us who are "externally beautiful" and those of us who aren't but have the
"fun-evening trifecta" (smart, sweet, and funny) — the luxury of being able to
relax and just be ourselves. Women (like men) have been told that if you're not
twenty-five years old, thin, tall, and...let's just say, "genetically blessed" (see "super-
model"), you have to work really hard to be attractive. However, a woman is least
attractive when she's working really hard at being attractive, an unfortunate Catch
36-22-36.*

*Our mothers all told us "You are a beautiful girl and the right man will
be lucky to have you." The key term is "the right man," because the right man will
be able to find a woman's beauty even when it's well hidden. You have no idea how
attractive to women that makes that man.*

CLOSE-UPS CURE INFATUATIONS

⚒

Infatuations are powerful short-term passions for people, things, or ideas. They're fun and they keep life interesting, but they can also lead you down some pretty strange paths. Take me for instance: I spend a lot of time standing in ice-cold rivers waving a long stick of bamboo over my head and I drive a 25-year-old car I just can't quite part with.

We all get infatuations. When it happens to you, move in and get really close, because the closer you get to something, the more flaws you'll find. But be very careful. Getting that close is big medicine, and either you'll find enough flaws to get over the infatuation, or you'll find that the flaws won't matter to you and the infatuation will morph into something far more powerful. Here are some examples of what I'm talking about.

In my early twenties, I developed an infatuation with golf, so I began playing all the time. However, the more I played, the less I liked a lot of the little things about it and, by my mid-twenties, I was cured and gave it up.

Then there is fly fishing. Once I developed an infatuation with it, the flaws included my own ignorance of entomology and how to tell why

I should choose one fly over another. Another flaw was my early inability to make a decent cast, but neither flaw made any difference when I felt that first wiggle and tug of life on the other end of my fly line. That wiggle-and-tug was a powerful juju and its mojo turned what had been an infatuation into a passion for the sport that has lasted since the 1970s.

Early in my first career as a photographer, I had just walked out of an extended meeting with the photo editor of a magazine I was freelancing for when I saw a stunningly beautiful woman walk out of the sales department. Instantly infatuated, I caught up to her at the elevator. Up close, she was even lovelier, but during the ensuing small talk, she laughed that she was still exhausted from the weekend. Naturally, I followed up with *"Oh? What did you do?"*

"Oh, like, you know, nothing," she gushed. *"Just partied down and stuff."* Just like that, my infatuation was cured.

On the other hand, I first saw the woman who would become my wife as she walked into a small shop. One glimpse and I was hopelessly infatuated. I got the first of a series of close-ups when I approached her and asked her to have coffee with me. She said yes, and by the time the check had arrived, the infatuation had deepened and I was hopelessly in love. Subsequent close-ups just deepened the feeling because, as I just pointed out, close-ups are powerful tools for resolving uncertainty.

An unresolved infatuation can complicate your life and become a heavy load that absorbs and diverts your mental resources. You want to keep it simple and travel light, so it's important to recognize one when you get it and even more important to remember that the way to deal with it is to get close enough to resolve it one way or the other.

CAROLYN'S COMMENTARY
DRAMA ALERT!

When your infatuation is with a sport or a hobby or anything that doesn't include us (unless, of course, it's another woman), get close enough to resolve your infatuation with it, but be sure to give the woman in your life equal time or she's eventually going to get dramatic on you. Women don't like being ignored or being second to anything else.

There's one other thing to be aware of. To women, this rule is very scary as most of us (I know I'm revealing a big secret here) have a touch of the "am-I-enough?" syndrome. This is an instinctive insecurity that stems from our cave-woman days when our concern was "if the hunter is not pleased with me, he'll find another woman to protect and feed and my children and I will die."

So, on some level, we fear that once you get really close, you may not be infatuated any more. When you find that you do like us, please let our inner Sally Field know "You really like me" so we can be happy and relax, at least a little. The results may be very ... rewarding.

SMART AND FUNNY WITH STYLE OUTLASTS GOOD-LOOKING AND COOL WITHOUT IT

⁓

"KISSIN' DON'T LAST, BUT COOKIN' DO."
GEORGE MEREDITH, 1926

If being smart and funny with style isn't more effective than being good-looking and cool, you explain to me why Sophia Loren (Google her if you don't know) married Carlo Ponti (Google again). The next time you see a ravishingly beautiful woman with a really homely guy, realize that it's possible he's got money and she's incredibly shallow. But it's far more likely that he makes her heart laugh and her soul sing in ways that are none of your business.

One of the great unfortunate truisms of this world is that beauty is only skin-deep, but ugly goes clear to the bone. It's a true — but incomplete — statement. Perhaps it should read, "outer beauty is only skin-deep, but inner ugly goes clear to the bone." When your own beauty is inner and comes from being smart, funny, compassionate, and generally interested in the people you meet, and your ugly is outer and comes from unfortunate genes and a face like a mud fence, you've still got a potent brew that can make you as attractive and cool as any rock star. If George Meredith had been a little more contemporary, he might have said, *"Flash don't last, but substance do."*

Of course, nothing is ever that easy. Like everything else in a man's life, being smart and funny with style takes work. We've already discussed that it's important to be the perpetual student so you don't spend your life as everybody else's pigeon. Now we learn that being the perpetual student also helps you be attractive to women. When you add funny to smart, you become fun to be around. Add personal style to that, and you could become downright enticing.

So let's talk about funny. Some people were born funny, but most of us weren't. I can't tell you how to be funny, but I can tell you how not to try to be funny. It's good to be able to tell a joke, but being funny as we're discussing here is not a matter of telling jokes. It's not quoting movies or body humor. There's not a seven year old in the world who doesn't think farts are funny, but, with luck, they grow out of it. Good humor is smart rather than puerile. You may not ever become hilarious, but you can cultivate wit.

Being funny in this context means being witty. In this context, it means expressing the connection between two or more insights or perceptions (the result of a working mind observing its surroundings) in a clever or apt way that makes the audience laugh.

For example, the English actor, Sir David Niven, (Google him) was presenting an Oscar at the Academy Awards when a streaker (if you're too young to remember streakers, they were naked runners) dashed across the stage and got a huge laugh. Not to be upstaged, Sir David smiled and said, *"Isn't it odd that the only laugh that man will ever get in his life is by stripping off and showing his shortcomings."* Woof.

Another form of wit is hearing someone say something, finding an alternate meaning for the words, and responding to that meaning instead of the one intended. But this is funny only if you understand precisely what was meant, the change that makes it absurd, and your audience recognizes both the change and the absurdity.

For example, two ex-Marines are talking about navigating the labyrinth of the Veterans Administration. One says, *"I needed a record of my discharge."* The other replies, *"Did you ask for a history of your unit?"* Alright, it's not exactly George Carlin-quality, but give it a minute and think about military jargon.

There! See? Funny.

Another example is *"She was so clean her sexual fantasy included Windex."* I have no idea who said this, but it's a wonderful play on the word "clean."

If you want to be funny by being witty, you can study the retorts of people like G.B. Shaw, George Burns, Groucho Marx, Winston Churchill and Robin Williams, but you have to start by being smart. Being smart starts with working at learning and understanding — figuring it all out and being the perpetual student. Once you've learned a little bit about how people think, you can start thinking about what they expect to hear and turning it upside down or inside out to create something absurd to surprise them. If it's clever instead of stupid, they'll laugh. Stupid is bad, but *silly,* on the other hand, can be wonderful. You'll find that a lot of smart women appreciate a silly streak in a man because it shows that he's confident but doesn't take himself too seriously. Remember, a lot of the guys who hit on smart women take themselves way too seriously.

Now we're going to talk about style. Building a personal style is easier than being funny. Style means doing things in your own particular way. There are a number of ways to acquire style. One way is to find a woman friend who has style (you'll know it when you see it) and ask her to help you find a "look" that works for you. Another is to look through magazines and find a combination of looks you like and make them yours. But no matter what you do, stay away from fads and trends. Looking like a bum on his day off or a ghetto punk is stylish only if you are one. Otherwise, it's just weak and unimaginative.

CAROLYN'S COMMENTARY
ATTRACTION ALERT!

❦

If you peruse any of the dating websites, you may notice that almost every woman's profile says "I want a man who makes me laugh." That just shows how important being funny is. If you aren't naturally funny, find a comedian whose style you like and learn his lines. When you've quoted funny long enough, some of it may rub off and you'll become funny.

Style, on the other hand, is wrapped up with confidence. Be happy with who you are and how you look and women will be able to see who you really are. Just be sure that what you're wearing reinforces the impression you want to convey instead of conflicting with it.

A man who really knows who he is and looks comfortable in both his skin and his clothes is well on his way to being attractive to women. If he can also make them laugh, let's just say he's well on his way to being on his way.

RULE FOR HAVING FUN #8

FUN AIN'T CHEAP
AND IT NEVER GOES ON SALE

⟿

This rule is actually less about having fun than it is about making and managing money, because without money, fun can be problematic. Yeah, yeah, yeah, I know. *"The best things in life are free!"* and *"Money is not the most important thing in the world!"* and *"Consider the lilies of the field...!"*

The best things in life are free, but it takes money to be able to carve out the time to enjoy them. Money is not the most important thing in the world, but the most important things in the world won't go out with you if you don't have any money. As for the lilies of the field, if you want to stand out in the hot sun and the rain and freeze your petals off every winter, fine, but shelter and real clothes cost money.

So, this rule is about making and managing money. You don't have to be rich, although if you're a member of the Lucky Sperm Club and were born rich, more power to you. But you do have to have some consistent way of making enough money and the internal fortitude to save enough of it to be able to live well, meet your obligations, and occasionally go have some fun. Like anything else, this requires a little forethought.

If you go to a university and learn a profession, fine. If you go to an industrial school and learn a trade, fine. If you decide that selling insurance or real estate isn't for you and decide to become a plumber or a garbage man or a handyman instead, fine. Just make sure you've got a gig that will pay you well enough to play because fun ain't cheap and it never goes on sale. You're going to want to go have some fun.

This rule seems to imply a devil-may-care attitude towards money, but that's not true. I think having money is a wonderful thing, but I think that being too acquisitive and spending every waking moment in its pursuit and wanting to be the guy in the graveyard who died with the most toys is problematic (read "stupid"). The smartest men I know figured out what "enough" money was for them, made that much and quit. Now, they're out living life and having fun.

CAROLYN'S COMMENTARY
PROBLEM ALERT!

∽∾

*To a woman, this rule can be problematic. If you **talk about** "needing only enough" money, a woman may hear "I don't need much" and may be turned off. If, on the other hand, you **demonstrate** that you have enough, she'll have a chance to see whether your idea of enough and her idea of enough match. If they don't match, you may have just saved both of you a great deal of angst and you may have also deprived some divorce lawyer of a huge future fee.*

But don't assume that you know what her idea of "enough" is. A man will tend to assess a woman and her situation, needs, and attitudes about money from afar and decide for himself whether or not he can support her in the style to which he thinks she might have become accustomed. If you're assessing a woman from afar, that means you are both probably out in the world at either a business or social gathering and she may have really worked at making herself look her best. Her best will probably look expensive and well-turned out, which helps explain why many smart, beautiful women sit home alone on Saturday nights. But until you've actually had the conversation with her, you have no idea what she thinks is enough. Make money, be secure in who you are, know that you have enough to have some fun, and then assess your other assets, lead with those, and allow the woman to do the same.

A GENTLEMAN ALWAYS ACTS AS THOUGH HE WANTS TO BE ASKED BACK

At first this rule seems like a simple matter of courtesy, but it's really more than that. If a lady offers you her attention and approval, respect her feelings. She has given you a gift and even if you don't want the gift, you still owe her respect and a little bit of gratitude.

Polite society should be just that — polite, and it should mean just that — a courteous, mannerly community of people. If a woman graces you with her attention, act slightly flattered by it. It costs you nothing, makes her feel good, and you have no way of knowing just how much raw courage she may have had to summon just to say something to a strange man. Be nice. Even when you can't get away from her quickly enough, there's no need to hurt her feelings by letting that come across. Be nice.

Unless!

Many, many years ago I was camped out in an infamous honky-tonk (now long gone) on East Colfax Avenue in Denver watching a table-full of drunken women laugh and drink and shriek. Most of them were harmless enough, I suppose, but one over-age-in-grade platinum-dyed-blonde was becoming increasingly shrill, profane, and offensive as she began to make loud comments about other patrons of the bar and then shriek with laughter. Finally, a grizzled off-duty Air Force master sergeant got fed up with her behavior. He ordered another shot of rye, downed it with one toss, and turned to lean his back against the bar, fixing a dangerous eye on the blonde. In a voice of command that brought the rest of the bar to silence, he said, *"Somebody throw a quarter in the juke box and play me a song or two."* His voice filled the room as he continued, *"I wanna dance and I wanna dance with a sweathog. I want me the nastiest, sweatiest sweathog in the joint."* Then he leaned forward slightly, extended his hand to the unpleasant blonde, and said, *"You'll do, darlin'. Do you wanna dance?"*

Okay, so that might have been a little bit over the top, but, Lordy, it was effective. I wouldn't have done it that way, but it was fun to watch. But what if that scene had been a little different? What if the blonde had kept her behavior within the bounds of polite society? What if she had walked up to the sergeant at the bar and had asked him to dance? What should he have done then?

Well, he could then have gone a number of ways. He could have said yes and taken her for a turn around the dance floor. Or, he could have said something like, *"Gee, I'd love to but this old war wound in my leg is killing me right now. May I buy you a drink instead?"* or he could have done any number of other things. What he could not have done was to have been rude to her or make her feel silly or anything else that would indicate that he did not want to be asked for a return engagement. The fact that she would have been operating within the bounds of polite society would have meant that he was obligated to do the same. She was not, so he was not.

A man considers the feelings of others and is as gentle a gentleman as possible without ever actually getting pushed into anything he really doesn't want to do. It costs nothing to be polite. Besides, she might have a really attractive friend — you just never know.

CAROLYN'S COMMENTARY

Of course, women appreciate a man who is polite enough and charming enough to internalize this rule, but to a woman, it has important implications for social engagements you attend as a couple. In couples, it's generally the woman who controls the couple's social calendar, but far too many guys accompany their women to a party or gathering or some other social function they don't really want to go to and behave boorishly, rudely, and stupidly because they don't really want to be there. If you don't want to be there and don't feel you need to support your woman, kindly have the balls to decline the invitation. If, on the other hand, you do accompany your woman, really show up. Don't embarrass her. Spend the time with her and don't waste it. Find a way to enjoy yourself, even if it's just by watching her. It's usually for only a bit of time and grown-ups can certainly find a socially acceptable way to entertain themselves in the company of others.

Rules for Having Sex

RULE FOR HAVING SEX #1
NO MEANS NO,
SO STOP AS SOON AS YOU HEAR IT

Bed is one of the few places two people can do anything they both agree to, anything at all. Either one of you can dress up as a sea captain or a ballerina, you can play games like "The Lady of the Manor and the Stable Boy," invite your friends, or get rowdy with a riding crop, hand-cuffs, and plastic electronics as long as everybody in the pile consents.

But "no" means "stop immediately" because somebody has stopped having a good time and bed is the one place you should be guaranteed a good time.

One reason to stop immediately is out of respect for the other person and her sensibilities, responsibilities, and psyche. The other is to avoid false recriminations and real blame when everything has been re-zipped, re-buttoned, tucked back in, and adjusted. Everybody involved needs to take full responsibility for having done what you've just done, but if you didn't stop when asked to, anything that happened subsequently *is your fault and your fault alone.* Putting yourself and your lover in that position just because you found it inconvenient to exercise a little self-control is really stupid and not something a man would do.

Sometimes, though, *"No!"* doesn't need to be said out loud. Sometimes it's implicit in the situation itself. If someone has had too much to drink to the point of incapacitation, *"No!"* is the operative command until she's back in control of her faculties enough to say *"Yes!"* and is <u>fully aware</u> of what she's saying. The absence of *"No!"* does not mean *"Yes!"*

If you still don't understand, go back and re-read the sections on integrity and contentment versus capacity, but whether you understand or not, whether you think she means it or not, whether she actually does mean it or not, *"No!"* means *"No!"*, and the unspoken *"No!"* can be the loudest *"No!"* of all.

CAROLYN'S COMMENTARY

This rule, when followed, gives women the freedom to enjoy ourselves without worry. Remember the multi-tasking brain of women? If part of our brain is concerned with our safety, or our ability to "escape," we will not have a good time in bed and therefore your time will not be as good as it might have been. Let us know from the beginning that you are truly there for us and that if we say no you will stop. You may almost never hear no.

EACH PARTICIPANT SHOULD FOCUS ON THE WELL-BEING AND PLEASURE OF THE OTHER

Elliot Gould once said, *"All a woman has to do to be good in bed is to show up."* Brother Dave Gardner used to say *"Gratitude is riches and complaint is poverty and the worst I ever had was wonderful."* I suspect they were both saying the same thing. If you want a partner to show up more than once, make absolutely certain she feels safe, feels appreciated and admired, and make damn sure she has a really good time.

In the beginning, though, that can be tricky. For years, the women's movement has told women that they're responsible for their own orgasms and other pleasures and that was certainly appropriate to the times. What that means to a man now, though, is that you stay tuned in to her, do your best, and if she wants something else or something different, you need to have made her feel comfortable and safe enough to exercise her responsibility to give you hints, clues, or, failing all else, explicit directions and ongoing encouragement. The nice thing is, that's a two-way street. But, if she doesn't have a good time, it's your fault, whether she helped or not.

Another two-way street through the bedroom is the one that leads to the issue of well-being, which means that each of you must make certain that neither of you get surprised later by any little viral, bacterial, or fungal bombshells, any tiny livestock, or any other kind of medical unpleasantness.

If everything you do in bed is designed to give your partner maximum safety and physical and emotional pleasure, and she brings her considerable resources to bear on pleasing you as well, the net result is that two good friends wind up trying hard to make each other feel really good. Sounds like a pretty good time to me, especially if you actually do want to be asked back to do something similar at another time.

If you can't have a good time under those circumstances, perhaps you can find happiness by settling down with a nice boy of your own faith. If that's what makes you happy, fine, but you're still going to have to learn how to be generous, gracious, and careful in bed in order to be able to go there on a regular basis with anybody you've ever seen before and want to see again.

CAROLYN'S COMMENTARY

Yup. Enough said.

WHAT HAPPENS "IN BED", STAYS IN BED. A MAN WILL NEVER BETRAY HIS PARTNER'S HONOR

This seems like a purely ethical issue, but when you start to parse it, it gets surprisingly complex.

First, there's the issue of privacy. It really doesn't matter whether you went to bed with a woman or a man or a sheep named Baaaaabara, she may not want it advertised that she went to bed with anyone, or maybe she just doesn't want anyone to know she went to bed with *you*. So, unless she starts handing out T-shirts that say *"Proceed without caution! I went to bed with what's-his-name and all I got was this lousy T-shirt,"* it's a private issue between the two of you and nobody's business but yours.

Secondly, she may be trying to control the information flow to protect herself from roving quick-hitters who would pester her for dates because they think they'll also be able to get where you just were.

Thirdly, that sort of information changes the way people view you both, with some people respecting you more and others respecting you less. That's the kind of effect for which you want a laser focus, rather than a shotgun approach.

Fourth, if you develop a reputation for not being able to keep your mouth shut about that sort of thing, you may start missing opportunities you'll never know you might have had. People of quality just don't want folks indiscriminately putting their business in the street.

Fifth, when you start bragging about your sexual exploits, the guys around you will assume you're lying because they exaggerate significantly when they talk about their own sex lives and will believe you do, too. The men around you will assume you're lying because they know that a gentleman always behaves as though he'd like to be asked back for a return engagement, and a woman who has just been characterized in a locker room as a bimbo or in a barroom as a slut will be unlikely to offer one.

Sixth, a woman may tell her most intimate friends every single detail, anatomical and otherwise (and she probably will because they do talk, which is why they're called "intimate friends"). But, a man *never* betrays a lady's honor.

Period.

CAROLYN'S COMMENTARY

On the other hand, if afterwards she is sporting a tasteful — and brand-new — piece of jewelry and is showing it to all her friends and telling them that you gave it to her, everyone will make certain assumptions about what happened and you'll never have to say a word. Making a quick stop at a high-end jewelry store has the same net effect as shouting the news from the rooftops. Want to write the world an intimate little note about what happened? If that one-word note is spelled "Tiffany's," they'll get the message clearly but you'll still come off as an honorable man.

RULES FOR
GETTING DRESSED

RULE FOR GETTING DRESSED #1

A REAL MAN CAN WEAR
ANY DAMN THING HE WANTS

A man dresses for comfort, utility, simplicity, and appropriateness, and does so with a strong, cohesive sense of his own personal style. In other words, he suits himself. The way you present yourself (the total package) tells others a lot about you and can be a way to attract the kind of people you want and weed out the kind of people you don't.

Of course, you can take this one so far that you may have to fight your way out of bars, fishing camps, and the occasional Home Depot. But, if you've got the aplomb to pull it off, you can wear a tutu, zoris with argyle knee socks, and a Warner bra. Why you'd want to is a fundamentally different subject and would require a different book altogether, but I've got a good friend who spent 15 years as a sergeant in the Special Forces and he occasionally wears his kilt to bars just because it's comfortable and airy.

The only time others should dictate what a man wears is when he accepts an invitation to a special occasion of some sort. Implicit when you accept such an invitation is your agreement to dress appropriately. Black tie means just that and not a seersucker suit or jeans and a sports jacket. Personally, I made a decision about 10 years ago to stop wearing neckties, with only three exceptions: if one of my friends wants to go to all the trouble of dying, getting married, or offering me a deal involving six or more zeros to the left of the decimal, wearing a tie to the ceremony is the least I can do and I'm always willing to do the least I can do. One other exception is an event requiring evening clothes (also known as "black tie" or a tuxedo) because I like wearing a tux. It's more comfortable than a business suit and one looks so damn dignified and stylish in a Fred Astaire, James Bond, emperor penguin kind of way.

So the rule is, follow the crowd if it pleases you, or go your own way and don't worry about it, but being inappropriate is rude. Otherwise, a real man can wear any damn thing he wants to.

CAROLYN'S COMMENTARY

As men will assess a woman by looking at the image she presents, a woman's first impression of a man's overall impact will cause her to assess whether or not he will fit into her world, and better yet, improve it. So while you're choosing your clothing and style, understand that the impression you give could cost you with others. Another way to put it is that the clothing you wear and the style you present are a filter that may eliminate you in the eyes of many women before you even open your mouth. Use that filter consciously and wisely.

ON THE OTHER HAND, NEVER WEAR WHITE SOCKS WITH A SUIT

~

... or dark socks with shorts. And for pity's sake, first, figure out which end of the baseball cap is supposed to face forward *before* you put it on. Secondly, take it off again when you go back inside. It seems like such a simple thing to decipher how a baseball cap works. It works one way when you're playing catcher in an actual baseball game. It's another thing altogether when you're trying to keep the sun out of your eyes, so it's hard to understand why so many guys guess wrong about it. On the other hand, a select few of them might be men already, like it whatever way they wear it, and they may not give a damn what I think.

So be it.

CAROLYN'S COMMENTARY

Absolutely.

JACK DALE is a writer; a corporate consultant specializing in start-up, turn-around, and growth strategies; an entrepreneur; an artist; an ex-photographer; and a public speaker. He lives in the Front Range of Colorado with a green-wing macaw named Picasso. Contact Jack at jdale@thecoderules.

CAROLYN STRAUSS is a published author, business speaker, and communication expert. She is a former model with the Ford Modeling Agency in NYC, and served as the CEO and on-air spokesperson for the Carolyn Strauss Collection, a line of women's apparel featured exclusively on the Home Shopping Network-USA. Carolyn teaches gender-based communication skills and personal presentation workshops for CEO's, management for companies of all sizes, and women's organizations. Carolyn Strauss may be contacted at cstrauss @carolynstrauss.com.

If you enjoyed this book,

please visit us at

www.thecoderules.com

www.ingramcontent.com/pod-product-compliance
Lightning Source LLC
Chambersburg PA
CBHW051727090426
42738CB00010B/2136